Live One Life

A Guide to Recovery from Trauma, Drama, and Other Addictive Behaviors

Dr. David W. Patterson

Presented in Dyslexie Font

David W Patterson

Contents

David W Patterson

Acknowledgements

Susan Patterson is my eternal best friend and I wish to express my gratitude for her boundless patience with me day-to-day and on this project. Without her love, keen eye for detail, and countless hours of editing, there would be no book.

Lori Beard is my friend, mentor, and coach who has been a patient, driving force in my life. She has taught me to own the process. Her fingerprints are all over my work.

• • •

My Recovery Team:

- Reid Walker would call me on my crap and bring clarity to my foggy path of recovery, 24/7.
- Nancy Logan lovingly helped me navigate my emotional landscape.
- Greg Schmidt was the epitome of unconditional love and service.
- Richard Larson taught me the real need for grace in all things.

My Super Smart Contributors:

Jessica Bartlett Chevrier, Kasi Heard, Lori Beard

Christian Boer, the creator of Dyslexie Font, thank you for your support.

Testimonials

"I am glad to work and collaborate with Dr. David Patterson. Having met him is evidence of God's hand in orchestrating the people that He puts in our path.

I have been amazed by David's vigor to help transform lives. His life's experiences have been for his good because, as a new man, he wants to provide support to other individuals in overcoming addictions. He empowers them despite the challenges and turmoil of their circumstances.

David's Compass Model is a genius masterpiece that roadmaps life's journey. I invite you to allow David to guide you in your path to victory so that you can Live One Life!"

Lori Beard
Certified Life Coach and Clinical Hypnosis Practitioner,
Creator of the 7Rs Method, Author, Motivational Speaker

• • •

"As Dr. Patterson so powerfully shares in this eye-opening, heart-touching book, 'Change is an inside job. We must start with ourselves.'

What makes this book so engaging is that Dr. Patterson speaks from experience. Painful experience; been there; done that; survived; here's how.

When the pain from his own life choices became greater than his fear of the proven solutions, he began his successful journey to recovery.

The honesty, humility, and hope found throughout this book can help anyone struggling with addiction or any weakness, to begin the battle again and win."

Tony Brigmon
Former Ambassador of FUN for Southwest Airlines,
Speaker, Author: "The FUNOMENAL Workplace"

• • •

"I broke my back in a fall and had many months of rehab and therapy in front of me. I experienced pain, weakness, a fear of the unknown and many "what ifs?"

David was forthright and positive. He is known for saying, "If nothing changes, nothing changes." He had dealt with his own pain and his personal experiences were inspirational and motivating.

I am not a "writer" but David encouraged me to keep a journal. I attempted it and when time had passed I looked back and saw the progress that I had made. It was wonderful and proved that my efforts were making a difference.

A true life coach can only bring to the table the things he has learned in his own life's journey. We believe he has found his true calling as he sets out on this journey."

Wayne and Marilyn Petree

• • •

"I was very unhappy with my life and couldn't find fulfillment in anything.

I was living a double life: pretending to be happy with my family in one city and acting out an addiction to pornography and sexual sin when I was working in other cities.

I began to lose hope. I wanted relief from the stress and the burdens I carried, but I felt trapped.

David listened like a true friend who genuinely wanted to help me. He taught me to be honest and accountable for my actions. He pointed out many ways that I was lying to myself and others and didn't let me continue rationalizing and justifying my thoughts and behavior in my distorted view of reality.

He gave me a list of things to do and I had to report to him daily. After performing the daily actions diligently for 40 days, I received an overwhelming sense of peace and love from God and an assurance that these were the feelings I could have more often. My life was going to be different and I wasn't going to be alone."

Client

• • •

"I was having trouble abstaining from pornography and masturbation. It felt hopeless as I never seemed to be using the right tools to get out.

David helped me with being accountable for my actions. He also walked me through the mental and emotional battle that was happening inside me that I didn't even know was there.

I realized David's technique was working the morning I sent him my calendar showing that I had abstained for 10 consecutive days. Looking at that number, I realized, it was not only a milestone for me but I also knew at that moment that getting out was possible. I had hope. I'm not scared that I'll be overwhelmed by a desire to indulge. I live in faith, not in fear and I feel freed from my past."

Client

. . .

"Dr. David Patterson has a rare gift of reaching the hearts of people through his compassionate communication in speech and writing on the subject of relieving human suffering.

He has gained this knowledge from years of first-hand experiences in overcoming the trials of life.

His wit and humor will lighten your heart with joy and laughter. Now his wisdom in this book can put you, a friend or loved one on the path to a better life.

God bless this publication."

Tom Waid
Addiction Recovery Program Group Leader

. . .

"This book is written from the perspective of someone who has prevailed extreme challenges. It compiles a variety of tools and insights to assist others overcome the traumas and dramas of life. An excellent and inspiring read."

Spencer T. Smith, RN, BSN

. . .

Introduction

I have learned that we are all recovering from something. You might ask, "Recovering from what? I'm not addicted to anything!" Really? Have you ever done something then realized it didn't serve you well; only to miss the mark and do it again and again?

"Addictions can include the use of substances such as tobacco, alcohol, coffee, tea, and drugs (both prescription and illegal) and behaviors such as gambling...viewing pornography, inappropriate sexual behavior, and disorders associated with eating. These substances and behaviors...harm physical and mental health and social, emotional, and spiritual well-being."[1] Would you like to gain control over your habit or behavior?

I made a deal with myself that I wouldn't start teaching or preaching "The Recovery Arts" until I was clean for ten years from my own issues and addictions. I now feel I can help others by sharing my story in this book and at LiveOneLifeCoach.com. I hope that you will discover something within this book that will help you find confidence, peace, and comfort as you recover your life.

You or a loved one's destructive behaviors or addictions may stem from some trauma or drama of life. This event might be something old or more recent. You may feel alone. Perhaps you've survived a traumatic childhood.

---

[1] LDS Family Services, 2005, p. v

Possibly you've been abused or you struggle with health or mental issues. Maybe you are homeless, in debt, divorced, or heartbroken. The list of life's challenges goes on and on, nevertheless, the steps of change for all of these conditions are the same.

If you implement even a few of the pure, powerful principles within this book you will be improved equally to your own efforts.

I wish I could say that the things I'm sharing in this book came to me in a simple, systematic way. That would have made this book much easier to write. No, the information you will receive had to be lived first. This is my personal chain of events, issues, and relapses. It has been hammered out link by link and yard by yard.

It is true that there needs to be order and that order will be determined by you. Don't we all want more organization in our lives? There is an eternal principle at play here. That is, you are exactly where you need to be to get started. As truths, principles, and techniques were revealed to me, I either accepted or rejected them. You too will have to make your own decisions as to what you are willing to do to improve your life. I am offering what I have learned and what unfolded in my personal journey. This is my book and it worked for me. I challenge you to assimilate what you can from these pages and test them in your own "Hero's Journey!"

I don't want to walk in front of you for I may be tempted
to pull you.
I don't want to walk behind you for I may be tempted to
push you.
I just want to walk beside you and be your friend.

Dr. David W. Patterson

Chapter One
The Problem

An argument had escalated between my father and mother. I tried to stop it. I grabbed him by the arm and said, "Why don't you leave her alone!" He snapped back, "Oh I'll leave her alone!" then stormed out of the room. I thought he was leaving. He then returned with a rifle and shot himself in front of my mother and me. He crumpled to the floor. I sent my mother to another room and then called the police. I remember kneeling over him and smelling the gun and the blood. I thought, "Good, he's gone. He is at peace. All those years of mental illness have stopped!" He was still, very still. My father never moved again. I sat there stunned, emotionless, staring at him. I was seventeen.

Let me take you on a journey that transformed my life to overcome my traumas, dramas and other addictive behaviors and that led me to write *Live One Life.*
Live One Life. Where did this title come from and what does it mean? While I was serving in my church in Dallas, Texas I was looking for a catchphrase or a thought disrupter to stimulate the thinking of my congregation, especially the youth. I wanted something that was familiar that I could riff

off of. At that time, a little acronym **LOL** (laugh out loud or lots of love) was everywhere in emails, texts, Facebook, etc. One day I looked at that acronym and something touched my heart, Live One Life, and I felt inspired to start using that idea in my sermons, classes, and counseling. I would share it with anybody who would listen. Now it has grown into my passion and practice: LiveOneLifeCoach.com.

The problem, as I saw it, was that many in my congregation, including myself, didn't always Live One Life. We try to live multiple lives. We attempt to keep the various aspects of ourselves in individual compartments or silos. Many focused on being one person at church, another at home, and yet another person at work or school. Even more damaging was we tried to be a different person in our own minds. I learned that these multiple roles that we created within ourselves were great diversions to the quality of our lives.

Relationship Alignment

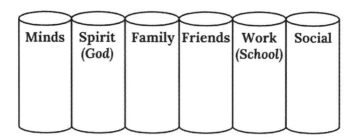

I see it time and time again. As people struggle with their issues and thoughts, their efforts to improve are derailed due to multiple distractions and unrealistic expectations. Trying to maintain these various scripts and roles in our life consumes our valuable time and energy. It can cause a lack of confidence and insecurity. This constant reformatting is mentally, spiritually, emotionally, and physically exhausting, not to mention the stress and chaos that comes when we mess up and forget who we are. Live One Life with purpose and show up fully engaged. I often quote the scripture, "with an eye single to the glory of God,"[2] as a reminder that there are higher ideals and that there is someone bigger than us. If we will look up and have the right goal, then we can calm and focus our life.

I have come to understand that we all need to work on this Relationship Alignment or what I call the "Integrity Model." We are here to be tested, learn to make decisions, and build relationships. It is my opinion that in this life we get to choose who we will be and how we will conduct ourselves. Yes, things are going to happen and we will be exposed to all kinds of good, bad, and exciting situations. It is our choice how we respond to these events that will determine how happy and comfortable our life will be. According to ancient wisdom, we will be accountable for three things: our thoughts, our words, and our deeds.[3] We

---

[2] Doctrine and Covenants 4:5

[3] Mosiah 4:30

should not hold ourselves accountable for the actions of others or situations beyond our control.

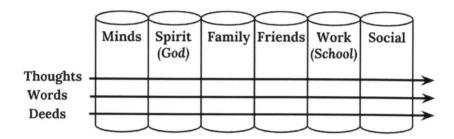

Knowing that you only have to develop influence and control in just three areas can be empowering. Are your thoughts, words, and deeds consistent in all of your relationships? Do you use the same tone of voice and gestures when talking to your spouse that you do when talking to your boss? Do you treat your family the same way that you treat your friends? Relationship Alignment is harmonizing your thoughts, words, and deeds so that you are consistent in all your associations.

As you go about mending or developing these relationships, it is helpful to know where to start. Knowing which relationships are the most important is pivotal. This is the "Relationship Hierarchy." In all relationships you must exhibit an abundance of hope and faith in each other. Let's put them in order of importance.

Relationship Hierarchy

1. Spiritual relationship: Becoming aware of what is greater than us. Coming to terms with the idea that there is a Higher Power may be difficult; however, I believe it is the most important relationship we can develop.

2. Family relationships: If you think coming to know your Higher Power is difficult, repairing family relationships can be excruciating. Nonetheless, these can be the richest relationships of life. Some of you may think you are ready to solve the complexities of the world yet you can't reconcile yourself with your brother's behavior at the last Thanksgiving dinner.

Now the disclaimer: Relationships with members of your family that require you to do immoral or illegal acts are not to be maintained. These relationships should only be considered after the inappropriate behavior has stopped and you are safe. If you are a victim of a family member then the appropriate relationship will be on your terms, if at all.

3. Employer: All honorable work is good. Until I came to understand this principle, work was work, and I was its victim. Here are the best lessons that I have learned to Live One Life at work. Be a specialist. Even if your title doesn't say specialist, perform your job as though you were a hired professional bringing your expertise to your job.

Honor your commitments with your employer; show up on time, be happily ready to work, and leave all your personal baggage outside of work.

Every payday is evaluation day for both you and your employer. Your employer has paid you and you have decided to stay in their employ. Or not! This attitude will serve you well and you will be in control of your career.

4. Community/Church: The opportunity to serve a Higher Power and your fellow beings. Service can be found all around you. Look beyond yourself. Service to others takes you outside of yourself, builds confidence, and provides a feel-good chemical dump.

The key to a confident and peaceful life is to have truthful, quality, relationships.

For learning to begin, a willingness to change must take place. Change comes through inner conflict; it feels like there is a struggle with your status quo. Aligning your relationships so that you act, talk, and think consistently in all situations will bring a new peace to your life.

Many of you have spent a lifetime rehearsing, nursing and cursing your past. These personal chants hold you back. Mental depression can come from living in the past. Believe that the past is a fixed experience; never to be changed. Trying to reconstruct or alter the past is pointless and overwhelming. Look at experiences as your own personal reference library. Honestly examine your past and see the cause and effect patterns that can aid in your decision-making today.

Growing up in one of Canada's main shipping hubs, Thunder Bay, Ontario, means I know what silos are. They are massive, concrete structures divided up to hold tons of different grains and dried goods. I have built some massive, mental silos in my time. You may have built your own silos too.

As an only child, I started building personal silos at a young age. I talked to myself in timid, doubting, and belittling voices especially during my early school years.

Reading was almost impossible for me. In the 1960's, in small-town Canada, the only solution for reading problems was to wear eyeglasses for either near or far-sightedness. By Grade 6, when reading became even more important, my marks started to fall off drastically to the point where I nearly didn't pass. When I failed Grade 7 twice, they just advanced me to the next grade. I continued to struggle and failed Grade 8 twice and was moved along again, this time to a trade school. Finally, when I had endured enough failure, I exercised what little control I had and quit school at the age of 16.

My Silos

To compensate for all this stress, anxiety, and failure, I developed a series of personal silos:

- A harsh, belittling and fearful self-talk silo for me
- A tearful, fearful, sometimes-angry-with-God silo
- A timid, victim silo with my parents
- My insecure, overconfident bravado silo with my friends
- A cocky, smart-aleck, hoping-to-be-funny silo for school
- An awkward and shy silo in social situations

All that self-talk and public posturing in multiple mental silos took a lot of energy and it didn't serve me well.

Twenty-five years later, a persistent ophthalmologist finally found my real problem. I remember he had to stand on his tippy toes to look through his scope to see the defect that had been missed by so many others. I had a rare type of vertical astigmatism and a form of dyslexia. All those years of chaos, struggling with reading and feeling stupid stemmed from a misdiagnosis!

Even today some of my thoughts, words, and deeds are still negatively influenced by my silos. I think this is true for all of us to one degree or another. Now, for the most part, my relationship alignment is solid and true. What you see and hear is what you get. At least that's what I strive for.

Trauma, Drama, and Other Addictive Behaviors

You may have picked up this book with the idea that you were going to help someone else and that's commendable; I admire your savior complex.[4] However, this book is not for other people. It is for you and me. We will discuss some difficult things here. I will be asking you to participate in an in-depth self-assessment. You may also think that this book is for those addicted to drugs or other substances. Remember, we all have addictive behaviors that are not working for us.

You will hear the phrase, "trauma, drama, and other addictive behaviors" over and over again. This is because trauma,[5] drama, and addictive behaviors pump feel-good chemicals into the pleasure centers of your brain. There are many harmful, negative actions and behaviors that you do daily that light up these pleasure centers. The sneaky thing is that these activities produce the same addictive chemicals that hard-core street drugs do. Your moods and behaviors are influenced by four primary chemicals created in the brain that affects it: dopamine, oxytocin, serotonin, and endorphins.

Here is a simple example of a perceived, pleasurable behavior. Have you ever been talking to a friend and heard

---

[4] A state of mind when an individual believes that he or she is responsible for saving or assisting others

[5] Bremner, 2006

yourself finding fault with someone? What was your motive? Truly, what *was* your motive? Did you find yourself getting excited or animated, perhaps laughing and joking at the expense of others? This is a diversion from a sad and boring life. It is a self-induced, chemical dump that manifests itself as a counterfeit feeling of joy and happiness. This feel-good activity seems harmless enough, but it is the same as the addict's need for chemical relief and distraction from his own life.

Traumas, dramas, and other addictive behaviors cause your brain to create a custom endorphin, dopamine, serotonin and oxytocin cocktail in an attempt to make you feel good. Thought, word, and deed decisions are a self-manipulation of brain chemistry and this is where you can begin knowing why you do the things you do. This understanding can even open your eyes to the idea that you could become addicted to these chemical dumps. You may actually be seeking out traumatic or dramatic events to stimulate the counterfeit "feel-good" drugs.

Many times you make yourself feel better by inducing a self-gratifying chemical dump at the expense of your loved ones and colleagues by engaging in gossip. How do you *know* you are engaged in gossip or idle talk? Because the person you are speaking about isn't there to explain or defend themselves. Gossiping has become an Olympic sport in our multimedia, polarized environment. This is an act of diversion or distraction from your own messy life. You have become an expert in self-medicating from your hurts and pains, whether they are big or small.

Later in the book, I am going to call upon you to do some personal investigation about what you actually think about. Examine thoughts, words, and deeds for their emotional payoffs. Dr. Phil McGraw's famous question asks, "How's that working for ya?"

Diversions can generate their own chemicals and they can also lead to addictive, alternative "medications" like chocolate or football. I know I'm on controversial ground here. Literally! I live in Texas where football is a religion. Not that there's anything wrong with football. But if you can list the full roster and stats of your beloved team and have a room decorated as a monument to this obsession, you might have a distraction addiction. If you are having trouble remembering what night the children's activities are on or what their current grades in school are, you might be distracted from that which is truly important.

I'm not here to find blame, shame or lay guilt trips. Even guilt trips can cause diversions leading to chocolate. What I want to do is share the things that I've learned that gave me, and hopefully will give you, the opportunity to analyze your situations and ultimately change your results. All this is done in an effort to find the good, better, and best in each of us. What I have come to learn is that we must take full responsibility and stewardship over our thoughts, our words and our deeds.

The elements that we have to accomplish this goal are our mind, our spirit, our emotions, and our body. It is my hope that through this book you can, as I did, become aware of these four tools to Live One Life meaningfully.

Chapter One

Do your best to set aside personal biases. Take a fresh look at your situations and challenges. You are no longer the judge, jury, and executioner! Play the role of observer and mentor. Please be firm yet allow for charity and grace. "Treat yourself like someone you are responsible for helping!"[6] Change is constant, not easy. Remember, all things come hard to a rebel!

---

[6] Peterson, 2018, p. 31

Chapter Two
If nothing changes, nothing changes.

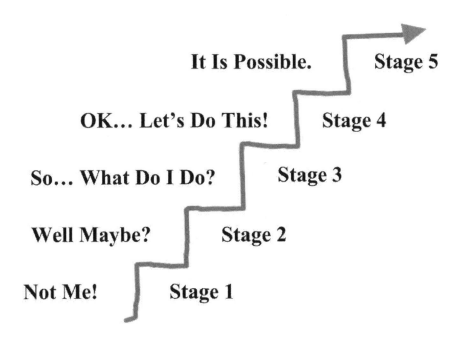

It Is Possible.   Stage 5

OK... Let's Do This!   Stage 4

So... What Do I Do?   Stage 3

Well Maybe?   Stage 2

Not Me!   Stage 1

Chapter Two

In my personal recovery, one of the most difficult stumbling blocks was the concept of change. I liked the idea of change for the better but without all the work that goes into it. Don't we all? What I struggled with was that for me to change; I must stop my current way of doing things and take up new, uncomfortable, even foreign behaviors. I found this to be the most mentally grueling game to play.

A study on recovery out of the University of Rhode Island introduced the now common model of "The Stages of Change."[7] Of course, men and women have been struggling with the complexities and fears of change for millennia; however my step adaptation of the Prochaska & DiClemente model is the one that I prefer.[8] Like all great life models, it is easy enough to understand although it may be a challenge to apply.

No matter what you are trying to change or recover from, be determined to change and then know what stage of change you are in. I like what C.S. Lewis had to say about personal change: "If you are on the wrong road, progress means doing an about-turn and walking back to the right road; and in that case, the man who turns back soonest is the most progressive man. We have all seen this when doing arithmetic. When I have started a sum the wrong way, the sooner I admit this and go back and start over again, the faster I shall get on. There is nothing progressive about

---

[7] Velicer, Prochaska, Fava, Norman, & Redding, 1998

[8] Prochaska & DiClemente, 1984

being pig-headed and refusing to admit a mistake. Going back is the quickest way on." [9]

Let us take a closer look at each individual stage. I will share my recovery story as we discover where you are in your journey.

Stage 1
Not Me!

In Stage 1 it's hard to even know you are in a stage. Sure, you have challenges like everyone else. That's just life. There is little to be done and you resign too quickly to situations. You're not thinking about change or even see a problem. If a family member or friend points out an issue, no matter how gently, you think they are exaggerating and attacking you. "Not me, I don't have a problem!" You even go to great lengths to prove it. I am sorry to say I have heard myself more than once arguing for my own shortcomings as though they were of value. It seems strange that we would argue and fight for our weaknesses even though I know firsthand that I have fought hard to protect my excuses instead of examining them. It was easier to hold fast to these familiar, destructive beliefs and behaviors rather than to let them go. Nevertheless, this "Not Me" stage is a necessary starting point on the path to Live One Life.

---

[9] Lewis, 1986, p. 22

Examine your assumptions or limiting beliefs and be honest even though it's not an easy thing to do. There is a natural side to each of us that will automatically employ the four stumbling blocks to change. One or any combination of these, at various times, has stood in the way of my recovery.

The 4 Rs: Reluctance, Rebellion, Resignation, and Rationalization

Reluctance: The inability or refusal to acknowledge that a problem exists. You may not be conscious or aware of the need for change or you may be in denial.

Rebellion: The resistance to being told what to do or what you need to change. True to the word "rebel," you refuse to change or acknowledge the need for personal growth.

Resignation: An accepting, unresisting attitude; giving up. You may feel overwhelmed by the need to change and resigned to the belief that you cannot change or grow which removes the drive to do so.

Rationalization: The beliefs that you know what is best for you and have all the answers. This is to believe that the problem is not yours but everyone else's. You may attempt to hide your true motivations and emotions by providing reasonable or self-justifying explanations for unacceptable behavior.[10]

After witnessing my father commit suicide, I couldn't get drunk enough, stoned enough, or fight and hurt others enough to make the pain go away. In this chemical-induced fog, I developed a new, false reality. In my distorted way, I rationalized that my father's suicide was entirely my fault and that through my rebelling and misbehaving as a teenager I had driven him to kill himself. I knew it and I believed that God knew it! I had killed my dad! I thought I had all that power.

By using the 4 Rs or stumbling blocks: Reluctance, Rebellion, Resignation, and Rationalization, I had effectively locked myself into this twisted reality where there was no hope, no cure, and no forgiveness. All I could do was push it down, bottle up the guilt, fear, and shame, and then mask it all with drugs.

Spinning the cycle one more time, I was telling myself with great bravado: "I'm okay; the world around me is crazy!" It was this "stinking thinking"[11] that kept me securely locked in Stage 1, "Not Me," for the next thirty years.

Over time, I resigned myself to thinking that my father had the problem, not me. I thought that I was okay and

---

[10] Prochaska & DiClemente, 1984   A great breakdown can be found here: www.breakthroughpsychologyprogram.com/stages-of-change-in-self.html

[11] Ziglar, 2000

could handle it in my own way. For years after, the sad joke that I used to minimize the severity of that event was that, "My dad was nuts, not me." If somebody suggested that I get help, the rebel in me would push back to make them stop. I had already been coping by using drugs and alcohol for years and it seemed like a viable solution to the trauma of witnessing my father's suicide. I've since learned that my reluctance to change was due to a lack of knowledge of what outside help could do. I saw no immediate problem for me. The rebel in me was heavily invested in my so-called "self-help drug program." I called the shots. I made my own decisions and I was not going to be told what to do.

I have heard many people speak about their traumas and dramas. I have read the studies and I believe that over 65% of those we meet are in a crisis; not just having a bad day but struggling to hang on. It is true we cannot make people change and that is why in this book we are not talking about other people; we are talking about you. We all need hope, understanding and positive change. Looking back, I see this included me.

Uncover the possible sources of trauma and drama that make up the complex tapestry of your life. This will take some heavy lifting on your part. Past events are impacting you today. It's difficult because you don't know what you don't know! Open your mind to the possibility that your thinking may be flawed and have a blind spot to the biggest traumas or dramas in your life. This is not easy ground to plow. It is natural to want to protect yourself. Many of us have been taught by well-meaning souls, some who were not coming from a good place, to just buck up and not to talk about our feelings and emotions. I agree we should not be whining at every turn but sometimes things in life are wrong and they need correcting. This is an inside job. Recognize and try to understand that it is your own Reluctance, Rebellion, Resignation, and Rationalization holding you back from changing your personal narratives. Congratulations! That's the start of Stage 2!

Stage 2
Well Maybe?

Recognizing your own challenges is not easy. It may not be immediately apparent that your pride, envy or even laziness is causing burdens. What events or situations, past or present, are stumbling blocks in your life?

_____

_____

_____

_____

_____

_____

_____

_____

_____

_____

_____

Chapter Two

Opinions are like belly buttons: everybody has one. Someone thinks that you could or should change in some way. A physician, teacher, member of the clergy or maybe even a judge has given their opinion recently. Let's say that some of it is valid. Consider what has been said.

Listening to others may be a new concept. I know it was for me because I thought I knew everything! Mine was the only opinion that counted. After all, no one knows my life as well as I do, so what gives them the right to comment or judge me? It's true that you have lived all the details of your life, yet that doesn't make you a competent, unbiased judge of the many events of your life. We are all biased and why wouldn't we be? We are the ones most hurt and impacted by our actions. I was too close to my issues to perceive them correctly. I had also mentally isolated myself into one way of thinking, never mind the distortion caused by the drugs. It was all that flawed thinking that held me fast in my downward spiral.

I had stuffed all my hurt and trauma down deep. I tried to talk over it and ignore the painful noise in my soul. I prayed to God for help! I then mustered all my courage of character and went cold turkey.

I got off the street drugs and alcohol and became active in my church. Being busy and involved in good works and serving others was an honorable distraction. Praying, reading the scriptures, and getting right with the Lord were very rewarding. Meeting Susan, cleaning up my life and getting married, and working hard on my own salvation was and is a beautiful and satisfying part of my life. I had replaced the street chemicals with a healthier, natural, chemical dump that came from good works. Researchers say the acceptance of God is perhaps the most effective tool to piece together a rich, full life[12].

All these things were good and righteous but I wasn't Living One Life. There was my other life bottled up and stuffed deep down inside. On the surface all looked well but in the 12 inches between my head and my heart I was living an anxious and nervous existence. I was still dwelling in multiple silos; living a false reality but I just thought of it as my life.

For the next 10 years, I had this new, although healthier distraction and addiction; a busy Christian life. All that activity at church, Boy Scouts, and community service was socially acceptable, even considered admirable, nevertheless, it was still an addiction. For a time, I could manage the damage from my past traumas and dramas with prayer, good works, and church service.

It was at this time that I suffered a back injury. I have suffered from chronic back, neck and shoulder pain due to multiple car accidents as a child, so physical pain was an old companion. This time I was prescribed painkillers and muscle relaxers. I rediscovered an old friend; drugs, and the temporary and artificial peace they offered! The drugs eased the physical pain and I noticed it also masked the emotional anxiety and calmed down my inner world. The results were quick and easy and who doesn't like that!

---

[12] Heinz, Disney, Epstein, Glezen, Clark, & Preston, 2010

Chapter Two

We were living in San Diego and my first prescription was about to run out. I could go to Mexico and for about a tenth of the cost buy prescription drugs legally and bring them back in bulk with no questions asked. I know, right! So, being a frugal Christian I went south of the border and bought a month's supply of my pills. You can see where this is going. Well, I didn't! I had forgotten, or more likely ignored, the addictive power of those drugs and my own susceptibility or weakness. Things slowly escalated over the months and years until I was taking a one-month prescription daily!

What I had effectively done, as they say in addiction recovery, is, "changed seats on the Titanic." "Changing seats" means I had given up one addiction for another but the ship was still going down! I had gone from illegal street drugs and alcohol as a teen to over-righteous service in the church as an adult, and then finally to a combination of prescription drugs and church service addiction. All this rationalization and unnecessary expended energy was because I had not dealt with the underlying issues of trauma and drama in my early life. I wanted to Live One Life, but I just couldn't manage it yet!

Perhaps there are some unresolved issues that are causing inner turmoil and discomfort in your life.

Some examples of trauma or drama are:

- Accidents
- Physical injuries
- Medical procedures
- Obesity
- Chronic illness
- Depression
- Natural disaster
- Sexual abuse
- Suicide of a loved one
- Illness of a loved one
- Victim of crime
- Domestic abuse
- Loss of faith
- Divorce
- Anorexia
- Lack of confidence
- Anger
- Anxiety

This sad, short list above is not exhaustive. We all know there is enough trauma and drama in this world to fill volumes. If your situation or event is not mentioned, it is still noteworthy. This list is meant to help stimulate thinking.

Chapter Two

Examine your past for experiences that may have shaped how you think. What are some traumas, dramas or unwanted behaviors from your life? Write them down. Don't hold back; there isn't time!

_____

_____

_____

_____

_____

_____

_____

_____

_____

_____

_____

_____

Warning: You are not going back to relive these traumas and dramas to use them to define or justify you!

Come to terms with the past in an effort to improve the future. This can be difficult! I call them, "My Hard Times." Sometimes these historic traumas become unhealthy elements in our current life. In your case, did you allow them to stay so long that they became old friends, or at least old acquaintances? They may seem innocent enough but have they become a part of the daily narrative, or worse, your identity? Do you refer to these past events or personal weaknesses often in conversations with yourself and others? Perhaps you bottle them up and push them down deep like I did. Now they are like the childhood monsters under the bed, invisible during the day, terrifying and larger than life in the still and quiet time at night!

It can be difficult to examine your inner world honestly because it has been shaped by so many events in your life. These experiences may have been hurtful and imposed. They can be unclear and hard to see that your current anger, greed or other addictive behaviors stem from traumas and dramas from the past. It is confusing to think that these familiar behaviors are formidable foes and that they have the strength to distract, addict, and if left unchallenged, even have the power to cause your own self-destruction!

If you are fortunate enough to have one or more of these pains, be grateful to have been blessed with a point of focus. With the capacity to make little adjustments within these troublesome areas, you have the ability to change these challenges. Thinking, feeling, and acting in these and future situations will determine the results in your life. Today determines tomorrow. Life is determined by choices. Whether you think life is meaningless or meaningful; you are right. You are the author. You choose how you are going to Live One Life.

Let's go back to those friends, family, or professionals whose opinions you may have resisted. The doctor may have said that your cholesterol is too high, get more rest or lose a few pounds. The teacher may have commented that you have a real skill in math but that the work lacks detailed support or if another class is missed you won't get course credits. Maybe the judge said that you can no longer drive or be left alone with your children. Is it possible that any of these opinions have merit? When those opinions come from a reputable authority, you need to consider them as valid. It can help you realize that change is necessary. This can get uncomfortable.

Change is demanding. The apostle Paul said, "We must become new creatures; old things pass away, and all things become new."[13] To not be the same anymore, we must change. If nothing changes, nothing changes! In the rehab vernacular, "If you always do what you've always done, you'll always get what you've always gotten." This old chestnut of wisdom may seem folksy or glib but don't be too sophisticated or resistant to receive knowledge placed at your feet.

---

[13] 2 Corinthians 5:17 KJV

Take an honest look at one of your old internal narratives. Rewrite it. Turn it from an excuse/weakness into strength.

_____

_____

_____

_____

_____

_____

_____

_____

_____

_____

_____

_____

_____

_____

_____

_____

_____

_____

_____

_____

_____

_____

_____

Chapter Two

You are not to be reformed, rehabilitated or re-educated. You must be **re-created** and this is an inside job! It always starts and ends with you. There is an old saying, "At the end of the road there is always a mirror."

Take a minute and review some recent opinions and statements made to you. Can you shine a new light on them?

_____

_____

_____

_____

_____

_____

_____

_____

_____

_____

_____

_____

_____

_____

_____

_____

_____

_____

_____

_____

Acknowledge your past traumas and dramas so that you can examine their validity. You may be giving them too much power. Consider your current desire to change and do some self-analysis. Take time to explore the potential risk or reward of change.

Chapter Two

In Stage 1 you were unaware of the problems. Now get ready for deeper exploration. Be willing to consider that there is a problem and that there is a possibility of hope. Stage 2 is referred to as the "Well Maybe?" phase. Even when you read about a trauma, drama or particular behaviors in your life, you may still remain sitting on the fence. Your problem or addiction is destructive to you and others but the need to change is not there yet. Being aware is not enough to make a decision to change. Decide to decide.

Be active in your own risk vs reward analysis. It's the change vs no change dilemma. Weigh the pros and cons and review the pesky 4 Rs again: Reluctance, Rebellion, Resignation, and Rationalization. Review past attempts at change and question why you failed. There are many who fall by the wayside at this stage. It is natural to highlight these failures, review them and make them bigger than they are. Avoid stalling out again!

Caution: Contemplative risk vs reward analysis can morph into "busy work" which gives a satisfying chemical dump. This busyness can go on for years using up valuable time and energy resulting in no change. This behavior reaps the consequences associated with it including poor health, strained or broken relationships, anxiety, and depression. Analysis paralysis is not the goal and I'm here to tell you that there is hope.

Psychologists use the term "cognitive distortions" to describe irrational thoughts or limiting beliefs. These perceptions are negative and many times you have falsely come to believe that your thoughts are reality. These distortions are so gradual that you don't realize that you have the power to change them.

Perhaps you have noticed some limiting beliefs sneaking in. Maybe this is the first time they have shown themselves. They stop you from thinking about resolving issues. They often include judgment phrases like: I am too thin, fat, tall, short, educated, uneducated, afraid, poor, and on and on.

See how this works? These limiting belief statements hold you back. They are false narratives that can derail you just as you are getting started. Carefully examine the content of your speech. Are you the one sabotaging yourself?

During my recovery I learned an acronym that would help me overcome these cognitive distortions.

MOANS

Must

Ought

Always

Never

Should

All of these words can be used to talk about duty and obligation or to give advice or instructions. They are also considered "thinking traps."[14] They trap your thoughts by

---

[14] Anxiety Canada 2015. Retrieved from https://www.anxietycanada.com/sites/default/files/resources/documents/Thinking_Traps_Examples.pdf

putting up false realities that seem absolute. When you tell yourself how you "must," "ought to," or "should" feel and behave, then you are constantly anxious and disappointed with yourself and with others.

Statements like "I must always be happy" or "I should never make mistakes" or "They ought to admit their mistakes," set up false or impossible outcomes that you can perceived as failure. If you find "must," "ought," "always," "never," and "should" sneaking into your vocabulary in a negative and judging way then STOP and examine what you're actually saying.

Please don't let this kind of language define you. You are far more than any one statement. You are the most adaptable, complex creature in the universe. You have unlimited potential with endless opportunities. I know there are people reading this and thinking, "I just don't know."

Sometimes when I'm talking to clients, I call them on their B.S. (Belief System). Were you thinking B.S. meant something else? You're right, it means that too!

This B.S. stifles positive change because it is based on fear, faulty logic, or straight-out lies. Change is hard yet necessary. Old thoughts and biases need to be uprooted and this is your work. Do something! Either act or be acted upon. Don't let life be determined by your defaults but by your decisions. Give yourself permission to make positive, life-changing decisions!

Stage 3
So... What Do I Do?

Many in the "So... What Do I Do?" stage are planning to take action and are making the final adjustments before changing their behavior. Much of the risk vs reward analysis has led to a decision to change. There may still be lingering mixed feelings about how bad your issue or behavior is. You might be looking to assess blame to some person or outside force that is responsible for your problem. Many of you have minimized your unhealthy behaviors thus fooling yourself to the real consequences. For example:

Family of Origin: "My whole family is hot-blooded. My father is passionate, with a short fuse, so I can't control my anger."

Environmental: "Everyone I hang around with swears. I have to swear just to communicate." "Swearing isn't that bad!"

Physical: "I'm in pain and the only relief is my medication."

Stage 3 is the time to consider working with a counselor, coach or mentor. It is also a good time to think about doing some general self-assessments that will unveil your strengths and weaknesses. I use both the **DISC**

Profiles[15] and the understandmyself.com process based on a personality scale known as "The Big Five Aspects Scale."[16] These are insightful and provide positive direction.

BEWARE! You can get caught up in deciding to decide, or analysis paralysis, sometimes for years. Refrain from wasting precious energy and time recycling through old life stories. You feel comfortable re-telling them. You know and believe them and may even receive special attention from others. They have served you well but these old narratives have gotten you to this place. In the addiction fellowships, they say, "Our best thinking got us here." *Your* best thinking got you into these situations! Start clean from where you are.

Anticipate problems that inhibit change. Entertaining negative thoughts will tempt you to ruminate longer, delaying progress. Push forward through this fragile time. Rely on your coach, team, and new strengths to begin making serious transformations.

Stage 4
OK, Let's Do This!

The fact that you are reading this book and have gotten this far should tell that you have the capacity to take on Stage 4. Personally, this was a difficult stage for me. I got all up in my head thinking about things that would

---

[15] https://www.discprofile.com/what-is-disc/overview/

[16] www.understandmyself.com/personality-assessment

make my life better; the type of things that could help me. I mulled these thoughts over and over again in my mind but would not actually take the necessary steps to bridge the gap by saying, "OK, let's do this," and take the actions to make a substantive change.

One of the best tools I have found to overcome this imagineering of my life was to write my thoughts down in a journal or diary. I am sure you have heard this before. I can testify of the strength of converting thoughts into written words. No matter how ridiculous or even unbelievable these words may seem; don't let it deter you. Push through, clear your head, and empty it onto the page. Be ready to act.

Beware: Don't overthink the act of writing thoughts down. To quote the old footwear god, Nike, "Just do it!" ☺ There is something magical about taking your thoughts and putting them down on paper. Writing creates a gateway from the spiritual world of thought to the physical world in which you must live.

Write and examine your thoughts and watch for patterns and common themes as they emerge. Look for cause and effect scenarios that reveal you may not be in control but remember that you do have choices.

I would like to introduce a concept that I have had to learn on my journey. Healing, repentance, and recovery are all overlapping and almost interchangeable as you try to initiate change. For some, this may be a real paradigm shift. You may think that recovery is for addicts and you're not an addict, so it doesn't apply. Well, in the past I too was rigid and judgmental regarding these ideas. For me, healing was for the sick, repentance was for Christians, and recovery was for addicts. I have come to learn that this thinking is way too simple. To use this book, you are going to have to become comfortable with the idea that you need healing, repentance, and recovery all the time. This concept is non-negotiable! Take it from one who fought it for a long time!

To some, the word repentance may sound too religious. That's OK, just set it aside for now and focus on healing and recovery. Please know that in this book we will recognize a power greater than ourselves.

At this point, you may be asking, "What do I do now?" "What actions do I take?" "What's next?" That's exactly what this book is going to explore. I hope you have honored your troublesome past circumstances. Honor them enough to write them down. Get a journal of some kind and record the things that define you. Try hard not to judge or justify your life; just record it in detail. Write down the good and the bad. This record is for your eyes only. Be fair as you write. Don't exaggerate, minimize or defend your behaviors. Be as impartial as you can. It will help you Live One Life!

Chapter Three
My Life Has Become Unmanageable
It is my hope that you will come to "know the truth, and the truth shall make you free."[17]

I was 50 years old when I took Step 1 of the 12 Step Addiction Recovery Program, "My Life Has Become Unmanageable."[18] I was sick and tired of being sick and tired! I had avoided and minimized my problems long enough. I had lost the ability to manage the physical and emotional pain and had denied the sad truth for too long. I couldn't lie to myself or to others anymore. My life and behaviors had become unmanageable.

I wish I could say it was my own good judgment that brought me to the point of knowing that I needed help. Perhaps 2% was my wisdom, however much of the need to change came from the stark reality of my situation. It was all too overwhelming. My addiction had grown over the years to unsustainable amounts.

[17] John 8:32 KJV
[18] LDS Family Services, 2005, p. 1

Chapter Three

For years I made monthly trips across the border into Mexico to bring back "my meds." It was legal but then that law changed. The Federal government closed that loophole and now my little trip was considered "international drug trafficking." With that avenue cut off, I had no other supplier. One alternative was going back to street drugs and alcohol and all the trauma and drama that would come with that life, never mind the legal risk. Truth be told, I did choose the alcohol for a while and I did explore my street drug options. These were paths that I had been down before except now I knew the price and it was too high!

I had never met with a professional to cope with witnessing the suicide of my father. Instead I learned to stuff the emotions and dull the pain, guilt, and anger with drugs. By the time I was 50 years old, I had been addicted to prescription drugs for 20 years, and sadly, I was comfortable in Stage 1, "Not Me."

I had a wakeup call when my friend, RJ, committed suicide. He had suffered from physical pain and depression for years. He tried to secretly "manage and medicate it" with prescription drugs. I was seeing firsthand that a good man's best efforts failed him! In a moment of clarity I thought, if that was the fatal result in his life, then suicide could be a possibility in my life. It pushed me to thinking, "Well Maybe?" my prescription drug use and my life were looking like they had become unmanageable.

Losing my friend was a traumatic event that was way too similar to my past. After my father's suicide, I would not go to see a professional counselor. With RJ's death, I realized that I had a blind spot to suicide. Perhaps this could be my fate. It seems utterly ridiculous now as I write this book yet I had never made the connection between drugs and suicide in my life. It's truly astounding how powerfully our minds can filter out the obvious when it comes to looking inward.

Now, here is where the suicide tragedy of my friend, RJ, comes into play. I admired and respected him. He was a family man, a professional, and a former Bishop who chose to hide his demons his entire life and self-medicate with drugs. He spiraled out of control resulting in him taking his own life by hanging.

I was rocked to my core as I attended his funeral, realizing it could easily have been me lying in that coffin. I watched his son who was about my age when I attended my own father's funeral. I wanted to reach out to him except I had nothing to offer. I was mentally, spiritually, emotionally, and physically bankrupt. Emotionally, I was still only 17 years old. All of my emotional maturing and learning had been stalled, even stopped, by a life of living in a drug-induced fog. After 33 years, I had come no closer in dealing with witnessing my father's suicide than I had the Friday night that it happened. After the police finished their initial report, I asked if I was free to go. I walked out the door, picked up my girlfriend and went to a bar, beginning the numbing, dumbing, and denial process that would continue in one form or another for the next 3 decades. Sitting at RJ's funeral, I knew I couldn't do it alone! It was all too much! What the hell was I going to do?

Chapter Three

Somewhere in my addict mind I found some clarity of thought. I must have because I took action, as we all have the opportunity to do in overwhelming times. So there it was, Stage 4. Within a few days I was confessing to a loving church leader who recommended professional help. The next day I walked into the Kaiser Permanente Rehabilitation Center in San Diego, California.

I'd liked to share a poem that I had copied into the front of my bible years before. It reflects how I felt at the time.

"He drew a circle that shut me out–
Heretic, rebel, a thing to flout.
But love and I had the wit to win:
We drew a circle and took him in!"[19]

I was hoping that rehab would be my circle.

In my addict brain and in my personal bravado, I vaguely remember thinking to myself, "I'll be done with this recovery program in two weeks!" I met with the intake counselor and did my best to explain my current state of addiction. It was difficult to minimize or justify the amount of drugs I was taking but the addict in me tried to maintain some dignity. I remember watching her face as I told her the amounts and frequency of my drug usage. She was a professional and didn't show any sign of shock. In some way, this was comforting to me. She restated what I had told her

---

[19] "Outwitted" by Edwin Markham

40

and asked again if there were any other substances that I was using. "No," I said, "I've told you everything." She went away and came back in a few minutes with a male nurse. They were kind and gentle yet firm when stating that they would need to start the check-in procedure. They were sure that a bed was available for me. A bed? A hospital bed? I didn't see that coming! That was never on my radar. With wide eyes, I asked her, "What do you mean a bed?"

Over the next 30 minutes they described in pretty stark detail what would happen to me if I went cold turkey on my own. The particular drug I had been abusing for 20 years was not going to let go of me easily. In simple terms, they explained that the withdrawal of this drug could cause seizures, which in turn could result in permanent damage or even death. They explained, "During the withdrawal from some drugs you wish you could die, but with this one, you can die." I remember this sentence stopped me cold. So there I was at a recovery crossroad. I was under no legal obligation to stay. No one had put me in this position except myself. Now I must decide to decide! Was I, maybe for the first time, going to treat myself like someone I cared about? Could I stop my self-destruction long enough for someone to help me?

I asked the intake counselor if there was any way I could do this without being admitted to the hospital. She said it was possible if I would commit to the full outpatient program; an all-day, five days a week regimen. I believe it was the strength of character I had gained from my confession to my wife and church leader that gave me the hope to stand and say, "Yes, sign me up!" The next day I committed to the full outpatient program that Kaiser was offering. It started at 8 am, for 8 hours a day, five days a week, with no end date.

I was now neck-deep in Stage 4, "Okay, Let's Do This." I met with the nurse and blood was drawn. I then went to the psychiatrist's office where he prescribed the medications I would need to take as I started the withdrawal process.

To be honest, I don't have a vivid memory of the beginning of my rehabilitation program. My rehab journal didn't start until 67 days after my check-in date; what most recovering addicts call their "clean date." Looking back, I am shocked that it took me 67 days to lift a pencil on my own behalf, especially with the support and encouragement I had. The first line in my recovery journal states, "Frustration is the story." I need to thank the Lord and the counselors at Kaiser for teaching me to write in my journal. Without them, I would not have the contents for this book.

I was fortunate to be in a rehab center as dynamic as the Kaiser Permanente Rehabilitation Center in San Diego. The therapists, coaches and mentors were on the leading edge of therapy and rehab for addictions. Along with the group meetings, we were encouraged to participate in anxiety and anger management classes, guided imagery, deep breathing, and yoga classes. All these revolved around the heart of the program which was Cognitive Behavioral Therapy (CBT).

I was introduced to different ideas and an entirely new way of thinking. I wish I could say I was open to these concepts. That wouldn't be true. Daily, I went kicking and screaming. I was entrenched in my old ways of thinking and I liked them! The pain of the solution seemed greater than the pain of the problem. I had a real chip on my shoulder. As hard as it was to believe, I was feeling a real grief for the loss of my addiction.

My first big obstacle, day two in rehab, was the idea of going into group therapy. My first response when asked to attend a group was, and I'm embarrassed to say, "Why do I have to sit and listen to a bunch of losers to figure myself out?" I now know that my own, personal hell was due to my banishment of compassion and empathy in my life.

Every morning at 8:30 am, after a 90-minute bus and train ride, I sat in a group that varied in size from 20 to 40 addicts. I listened to them and they listened to me. For the next two years, every weekday morning this was my group. The size had grown and shrunk, members had come and gone, and yes, some even died. We shared thousands of stories, experiences, and tears, and slowly over time I was changed.

Chapter Three

In addition to the morning group, I participated in two or three other classes each day. These core classes developed new tools or skills to put in my toolbox.

They included:
- Cognitive Behavioral Therapy (CBT)
- Dialectical Behavior Therapy (DBT)
- Guided Imagery and Meditation
- Yoga
- Narcotics Anonymous 12 Step Program

In the beginning, if I had known how long and how hard it was going to be, I may not have started the program at all! In the first few pages of my little Moleskine journal, I described what I had been doing for 67 days. I had been going to either two Alcoholics Anonymous (AA) or Narcotics Anonymous (NA) meetings daily as well as attending two core classes at Kaiser Rehab. I was also required to meet with a therapist once a week and a psychiatrist once a month.

I heard in the addiction meetings, "The stronger you start, the longer you'll go." In many of the Anonymous Fellowships they had what was called a 90 in 90 rule; that's 90 meetings in 90 days. This was a tried and true method for setting a good foundation. It's been said many times by addicts working their recovery that, "When you hit rock bottom, you're in a great place to build a solid foundation." In my case, I had finally admitted the truth that my life had become unmanageable and that I needed help in overcoming my addiction. I was all in and went to 2 meetings a day for 120 days and then 1 meeting a day for the next 18 months.

There are many good reasons for a newcomer to attend 1 meeting a day or as many meetings as possible. At this fragile time in recovery you need the consistency and fellowship of others. You need to learn the 12 Steps and develop new habits and friendships to replace those unwanted habits and so-called friends you had in addiction. I now consider those meetings as my dialysis. They were a matter of life or death and as important as renal dialysis is to the kidney patient. As I write it now, it looks plain and simple; however that was not the case then. Referring back to my recovery journal, this quote summed up my attitude at the time. "Now that my last 'calming tool,' drugs, were off the menu; let the wreckage begin." As Maximus said in the movie, "Gladiator," "On my command, unleash hell!" And this was hell.

I was the author of this mess and now it was time to rewrite the next chapters of my life. My journal went on to describe, in scary detail, how much I hated going to rehab. I used to love being by myself; now I was afraid to be alone. This was hell and the only way out was through it.

My therapist suggested that I start calling myself David. In the past when asked which I preferred, Dave or David, I had no opinion. I didn't care what people called me. Now it seemed important to have a clear identity; David. Again from my journal, "Today I thought I should work on the actual polishing of David and stop just applying a veneer."

Chapter Three

My commitment of going to rehab daily was starting to teach me that in recovery, every part of David was on the table. My spiritual beliefs, my values and my opinions all needed to be examined and re-evaluated, and all that work was to be done by me! When it came to change, nothing was off limits. The way I thought about everything had to be evaluated. I could not leave any stone unturned. I had to take full responsibility for everything. I could not assess blame to others. In recovery, it was called, "cleaning my side of the street."

One of my first big takeaways was how many addictions there were. Unfortunately, almost without exception, they all ended in the same way. Our lives had become unmanageable. Granted, most of them were what you would expect like alcohol and drugs, both prescription and illegal.

I was amazed at the list of other damaging and unwanted behaviors and addictions: overeating, sex and pornography, abuse by family or others, personal drama and anger, digital device addiction, playing video games, workaholism, exercising, spiritual obsession, physical pain, cutting, and compulsive shopping. I was awestruck as I sat in the group sessions and listened to the stories of pain and destruction. It was truly amazing how we all had used behaviors and substances to develop defective coping skills to try to make our world a little better. I had never made the connection before that those traumas and behaviors could activate chemicals in our brain that would act as a gateway to even more self-destructive habits.

The haze was slowly starting to clear in my brain. The drugs that the psychiatrist had prescribed didn't replace my old high; these drugs had real work to do. The new prescriptions for withdrawal and antidepressants helped ease mental, emotional and physical symptoms.

Note: There is no shame in seeking professional help! Following a professional's guidance is not a weakness!

Even with all this help, it felt like I was being laid out raw for the whole world to see. All of me was on the table to be dissected, examined, and evaluated. I felt like I was the patient, victim, and attending physician all in one. There was good news and bad news. The good news was that for the first time in my life I was consciously taking full responsibility for me. The bad news was that for the first time in my life I had to take full responsibility for me, and I was in way over my head.

This was a challenging time. I had to examine every element of my life. I questioned how I thought and felt about everything: how I took care of my mind, body and even my spiritual beliefs. I had to figure it all out! All my values and beliefs, limiting or otherwise, were up for grabs.

I was starting to understand why the butterfly was commonly used as a symbol of recovery. For this to work, I had to have a total transformation or metamorphosis. I was now the liquid in the cocoon that was being transformed a little each day. I thought this was what it meant in the Bible when it said, "And be not conformed to this world: be ye transformed by the renewing of your mind, that ye may prove what is good."[20]

We must all find our way through the bad and difficult times. I was proving to myself what was good.

I was in this place willingly yet most days it didn't feel that way. It was a daily fight. I found it difficult to focus as all this new information flooded in from every direction. My old habits of avoidance, distraction or just plain ignoring my problems were not serving me well. There are many of us that are in the depths of our own creations, looking for a better way however I was not alone and neither are you.

As the fog was slowly lifting, I felt a little better. I sensed the need for new, good, sound content for my brain. For the first time I saw a real need for wisdom. "Educate yourself, David!" And like a good addict, I got obsessed with this idea. I went to the public library and checked out audio books. With my dyslexia and insufficient focus due to my recovery, audio books became comforting to me and a great way to learn.

One day I was listening to a book by Gordon B. Hinckley entitled *Standing for Something: 10 Neglected Virtues That Will Heal Our Hearts and Homes.* In his book he said we should read and study from the best books. Gordon described his home when he was a little boy and that

---

[20] Romans 12:2 KJV

his family had a full set of the *Harvard Classics*[21] in their library. I had never heard of the *Harvard Classics* so I went to the internet to see what I could find. I won't take the time now to bear my testimony of the greatness of the *Harvard Classics* although I highly recommend everyone read them.

I was unemployed and money was tight so I put a shout out to the universe for anybody who had an old iPod that I might borrow. My intentions were to download books and articles to listen to. A dear friend heard me and gave me a second-generation iPod. Shortly thereafter, because I was looking, I discovered LibriVox.org. That was a life-altering pivot for me. I could listen to many of the *Harvard Classics* for free!

When they were published in 1909, the *Harvard Classics* were known as *Dr. Eliot's Five Foot Library*. Now through the generosity of a friend who gave me an old iPod and the many volunteers on the internet, I could listen to the works of Franklin, Penn, Plato, Marcus Aurelius, Milton, Emerson and Confessions of Saint Augustine to name a few. I found this literature to be more helpful than the more modern books. The ancient writings seemed, in my opinion, to be more character and value-based. They spoke of life's foundation stones of integrity, humility, fidelity, temperance,

---

[21] "The Harvard Universal Classics", originally known as "Dr. Eliot's Five Foot Shelf," is a 51-volume anthology of classic works from world literature, compiled and edited by Harvard University president Charles W. Eliot and first published in 1909 (Wikipedia)

courage, patience, modesty and the Golden Rule.[22] I was clearing my brain of toxic substances and toxic thinking and replacing them with the writings of great minds. Due to my dyslexia I had only passed the sixth grade however my wife, Susan, said that now was the beginning of my classical education.

The task of rehab went as well as could be expected although the work of day to day life was getting complicated. I was unemployed and the great recession had just started. We got caught underwater with three investment houses, a car being repossessed, and we were now $200,000.00 in debt. The final test came when a routine physical exam found a malignant melanoma or skin cancer and I needed surgery within days.

Thank heavens I was surrounded by recovery professionals! They pointed out to me that my life had been saved by the early diagnosis. I know that my old way of thinking and my natural self would have never come to that positive conclusion under any circumstances. Even with all those troubles, I had glimpses of a sense of hope. Granted, most days I was buried in frustration, depression and anxiety; still hope would appear every few weeks. I have learned that you can ride a little hope for a long time if you nurture it but at this stage of my recovery, the only way I was even aware of hope was when it was pointed out to me by professionals, friends, family or My Team.

---

[22] A rule of ethical conduct referring to Matthew 7:12 and Luke 6:31: do to others as you would have them do to you

Chapter Four

My Team

"Sometimes the only thing you could do for people was to be there."[23]

For some reason, far beyond my wisdom and capacity at the time, I felt moved to assemble a team; a few trusted capable individuals that I could turn to in times of chaos during my recovery. Whether you are making small, incremental changes or about to upset the entire apple cart, it is paramount to have participants who want the best for you. Choose people that will challenge you and your thinking. I'm not talking about friends or companions that have the same general weaknesses as you do. No, I'm talking about caring people of a higher standard. These are people you respect and can help make positive changes.

---

[23] Sir Terence David John Pratchett OBE (28 April 1948 – 12 March 2015)

Chapter Four

At times of change and recovery you can be weak and vulnerable. Choose trustworthy people of character that won't take advantage or participate in your traumas and dramas. You can derive a great deal of strength and personal power from a team. To benefit from the relationships of others, take the time and make the effort to assemble the team. You may feel a sense of urgency but be patient. Finding the right people is more important than filling some arbitrary roster.

The first member on my team was my wife, Susan. This might seem like a no-brainer but if Susan was the source of my trauma or drama, she might not be the right team member. I knew she would not abandon me. She had covenanted with God to stay with me and she is a powerful woman of character who takes God at His word. She is a person whose covenants and commitments are real.

When you're ready to be totally honest, then your spouse might be a good team member even though this may feel uncomfortable in the beginning.

As a word of caution, if they are a victim of your infidelity or abuse, they're not a good team member. They need to be given their own space, time, and safety to heal.

Don't encumber a spouse or any others on the team with information, details or responsibilities that are not theirs to bear. Your stuff is your stuff to deal with and it all belongs to you! Remember, these are not paid professionals. They are family and friends you've asked to hear your ideas on how you might improve.

My second team member was Reid Walker, a friend of mine from church. He was a cop (a detective) and I knew he would call me out on my crap. I loved and respected him, and he loved and respected me. Most importantly, he would clearly speak the truth when I needed to hear it! I looked to him for clarity.

The third team member was Nancy Logan, a woman with whom I had volunteered with in the Boy Scout program. She was the loving, gentle, motherly type. I say motherly because she had that ability to cut right to the heart of an issue, call you on it, and then lovingly steer you in the right direction.

Next on the team was Greg Schmidt, a man that I knew from another congregation. He was a true servant of the Lord and would do anything for you, day or night without whining or questions asked.

The last one was my ecclesiastical leader, Richard Larson. I needed to know God's opinion on what I was doing. I wish I could take credit for coming up with the idea of assembling my team. It came in those vague 67 days of my early recovery, the days that I have little memory of, so I have to give this one over to God's direction and His grace and mercy.

I found that with five members there was always someone available. It gave me options while it protected them from being misused or abused over the years. My team was made up of people I saw on a regular basis and consisted of both males and females. This gave me a broader perspective.

Caution: With having members of the opposite sex on your team, you must exercise appropriate behavior. For example, a man and a woman who are not married to each other should never meet together privately or discuss things of a sexual nature. These types of issues must be taken up with trained counselors or therapists. No matter how innocent or helpful you think this might be, this is inappropriate behavior and you are playing with fire that can lead to greater complexities and heartbreak. This is especially true when your recovery may have made you weak or vulnerable.

All that being said, one of the greatest strengths that come from having a team is accountability! Choose to be accountable to them and most importantly, choose to be accountable to yourself. It's natural to want to hide and isolate the things we're not proud of or some behavior or activity that we've convinced ourselves is shameful or abnormal. I highly recommend accountability partners. We can't do it alone. Thinking we are accountable to just ourselves is never healthy. For us addicts, this, "go it alone" thinking may have contributed to our predicament. As for the rest of us, our "go it alone" or "I got this" attitude may be plain old everyday pride. Do not succumb to these destructive ways of thinking. Suck it up and assemble a team! You may want to ask the universe to help you with this process.

I was blessed because my team consisted of members of a Christian faith, so we all had a mutual understanding. We shared common goals and a love of God. My team was obedient to the council in John 15:12, "This is My commandment, that you love one another as I have loved you."[24]

Being of the same faith is not a requirement although I think common values are helpful. They weren't addicts. That's not the common ground I was talking about. If you don't have a church or organization of like-minded people perhaps you could look for something that you're passionate about and requires you to improve yourself.

While I was in rehab there was a single, middle-aged woman who had suffered a great deal with all that can befall a woman addicted to drugs and alcohol. It had nearly killed her twice. She was not affiliated with any faith or religion. She had no family or friends left, so she found an organization that rehabilitated baby seals. She threw her full effort into her chosen purposes: working on her recovery and showing up on time to nurse the baby seals. This was enough to give her some meaning and stabilize her life so that she had a better chance at recovery.

The search for a team or organization will likely be difficult and uncomfortable. That's okay. None of us are thrilled about getting outside of our comfort zone; however it is worth the effort to share our honest thoughts and feelings with others. Never mind others; I had a hard time being honest with myself!

Whatever you are trying to overcome, the new team should not be actively engaged or suffering from the same

---

[24] NKJV

situations. You don't need a team of accomplices. If you are embroiled in family dramas then befriend someone who has a stable home life that you can emulate. You think we would naturally know that, yet we don't! It is more likely that we will find someone in worse shape than we are and then commiserate on our common problems. I have learned not to get financial advice from an advisor who was selling goldfish at Walmart last week and lives in their parent's basement.

I worked hard putting my life back together mentally, spiritually, emotionally and physically. I was clean from my addictions for 10 years before writing this book. This foundation of strength in recovery has given me the skills and confidence to share my personal path.

In this time of global communication, you can find people, support groups or programs that can help with problems or weaknesses you may have, however it is going to require effort on your part. Get started! Google whatever issues you might have. There are hundreds of anonymous fellowships and meetup groups online and most of them will have support meetings nearby. Online support is a great way to easily get started. Consider LiveOneLifeCoach.com to be a part of your team. However, as good as online coaching and mentoring may be, you still need face to face interaction with trusted brothers and sisters in arms!

Choosing a team is hard work! It's difficult and humbling to reach out and surround yourself with people that will challenge you! It will take courage and good judgment.

A note of caution: Please be careful and protect yourself from those who might do harm or who would pity you.

You want quality people who:

1. Want the best for you and from you
2. Are striving to lift themselves up
3. Who will support you in your efforts

I remember my first recovery. I was 20 years old. I met Susan, my wife-to-be, and she had much higher standards than what I was living. As we began dating, I tried to blend my old street gang friends with my new life.

At that time I believed I would not live past the age of 27. I was living a lifestyle that would fulfill that self-imposed destiny. I had run with my gang of four all over the country for the past five years sharing everything we had: drugs, cars, and money. These were some of the toughest, most ruthless people I have ever known, and yes, I was their leader.

I thought we were loyal. I was shocked at how quickly my old world fell apart. In less than a week, the friends that I had lived with, fought beside and probably would have died for were gone. When they were exposed to my new world of proper behavior, no drinking, no drugs, and no smoking, they could not stand it. The only thing that they were exposed to was a little order and my new, slightly organized, semi-righteous way of living. That new light was too much for them!

Chapter Four

Sometimes when making a great change in your life and "becoming a new creature," you may have to stand alone, at least for a while until you can find family or friends that will stand by you and lift you up. Remember, that person needs to be strong in character to be able to help you, so find qualified people. The Good Samaritan[25] was not weak, needy or broke! He offered assistance from a full cup. Surround yourself with those who have the capacity and competency to help.

---

[25] Luke 10:25–37 KJV

Chapter Five

Doodle to Compass

When I was young, I remember working in the garden with my grandmother on the family farm. I was regaling her with some new and wonderful thing as little boys do. I don't remember what that was now although I do remember what she said to me. "There is no new thing under the sun.[26]" I briefly challenged her on that. She just said, "It's all been done before," and went on to teach me that all important things had been done by many others in ancient times.

I don't know if I completely believed her but to my knowledge she never lied to me, so I guess I was OK with that. At home I had heard my mother say many times, "There's nothing new under the sun," so I guess grandma must've taught this to mom as well.

It wasn't too long after that, I was sitting in Sunday School Class and the teacher quoted, "There is no new thing under the sun." I thought she must know my grandmother!

---

[26] Ecclesiastes 1:9 KJV

Chapter Five

Years later on another Sunday, the Bishop was preaching from the pulpit and quoted wise, old King Solomon. From Ecclesiastes 1:9 he read, "There is no new thing under the sun," and I thought to myself, King Solomon's been working in the garden with grandma!

There are no new principles in this world; they just come in different packages. What I give to you in this book are timeless, transferable principles.

Above is the compass model that I doodled and over time it has brought clarity, meaning and helped orient me as the fog was being lifted during my recovery.

Symbols like these have been used for thousands of years to give guidance, vision and direction. This symbol became a director or touchstone that helped me focus my thoughts and actions. Its' design is based on medicine wheels used by indigenous peoples all over the world. At this point some of you may be having apprehensions of this method of focusing thought. Do your best to push through any biases you may have. Open yourself to wisdom structures that have been helping guide people for generations.

I first came across them when I was a boy in Northwestern Ontario, Canada. I saw mostly Ojibway, Cree and Chippewa wheels on drums, canoes and souvenirs. While on vacation in the western plains, my wife and I came across a replica of a Lakota medicine wheel. We enjoyed the peace and reverence we found there as we stood in that humble ring of stones. It was only 30 feet across, yet it left a powerful impression. These symbols or some version of them have re-appeared time and time again throughout my life.

Over the centuries there have been many meanings given to the four quarters or quadrants of the medicine wheel.

Some are: the four directions (north, east, south, and west), the four seasons, and the four races of man made by the Creator. The most common are the elements that make each of us up. These quarters are our mind, spirit, emotions, and body which are the faculties we have control over or at least have some influence.

Many religions and wellness programs have adopted the medicine wheel to teach their principles. It is also the inspirational source for the "Wheel of Life" and the "Talking Circle" adapted and used in modern group therapy.

Chapter Five

I still like the 13,000-year-old version that I saw as a little boy in Canada. The Museum of Ontario Archaeology[28] explained that 13 millennia ago the Anishinaabe people saw the quadrants of their medicine wheel this way.

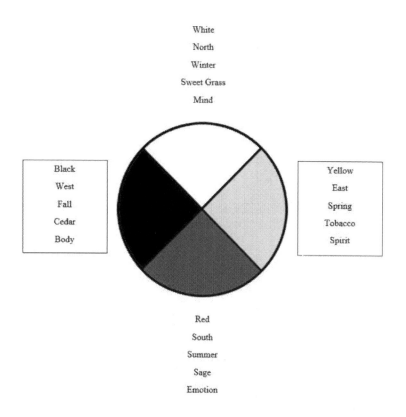

White
North
Winter
Sweet Grass
Mind

Black
West
Fall
Cedar
Body

Yellow
East
Spring
Tobacco
Spirit

Red
South
Summer
Sage
Emotion

---

[28] Ireland, 2015

You may be wondering what this has to do with Live One Life or recovery. As I was reading the wisdom literature of the ancient philosophers in the *Harvard Classics*, the old medicine wheel vision would not leave me alone. I was not aware that this symbol had been a part of the fabric of my life until I found it doodled in the margins of my recovery journal multiple times! I knew it held an answer although I struggled to make the connection to my current situation.

All of my beliefs and values were up for examination and possibly everything needed to change. As I was reconstructing myself during recovery, I wanted to build on a foundation of sound, time-tested principles. I had the idea that the application of simple principles could produce clarity and profound effects in my life.

It wasn't until I read in Mark 12:30 that it all came together for me. "And thou shalt love the Lord thy God with all thy **heart**, and with all thy **soul**, and with all thy **mind**, and with all thy **strength**: this is the first commandment."[29]

The idea struck me! God would not set us up to fail. If this is true and is the first commandment, then I must have some influence or control over my heart, soul, mind and strength. For the first time I saw four distinct areas in which I could work on and be accountable to myself, God and others. This Bible verse aligned with the four quadrants of the medicine wheel and the ethics of the ancients in my *Harvard Classics*.

---

[29] KJV

Chapter Five

I used the *Webster's 1828 American Dictionary*, which many academics agree is a helpful tool when trying to interpret and find meanings in the *King James Version of the Bible*. (Remember, I'm an obsessed addict in recovery looking for absolute truth and the best ancient wisdom.) By using the 1828, I interpreted heart to mean emotion, soul to mean spirit, and strength to mean body. There it was; a model consistent with the medicine wheel. This was my epiphany! I now understood the names for the 4 quadrants of the medicine wheel and how they related to the scriptures. These were areas with which I could make daily improvements. I found hope and peace in this model. Every day I find it gives me meaningful direction and purpose.

Live One Life Compass Model

From time to time I guest lecture on this model at a Divinity School in Dallas, Texas. I was asked to present my Compass Model to the graduating class of soon-to-be pastors. I shared with them the challenges of dyslexia and how it has made me a more visually graphic person. At the conclusion of the class one of the students remarked openly for all to hear, "Thank God for your dyslexia because now we all have your Live One Life Compass Model." I had never thought of thanking God for dyslexia until that moment. I do now! When I was first doodling or designing my compass, I certainly wasn't trying to create something for others. I was just trying to make sense of my own recovery and bring some clarity to my own pathetic situation.

The Circle

The circle is a nod to the wheel of life that is so common in many beliefs. To see these, do a simple Google search and you will find old and new applications of this ancient symbol. Circles represent strength, wholeness and unity.[30] We all instinctively know the never-ending cyclical nature of a circle. Our entire environment is described in terms of cycles and circles: the sun's path, the changes of the seasons, even our own mortality.

The circle is an easy doodle. Pick up a pencil, draw a circle a few times and there you have a good representation of the endless potential of your life right before your eyes. Now what do you do with the whole of it? How do you fill it or surround it with fulfilling and meaningful things? My compass will help you daily with those questions and many more.

The Arrow

Arrows have been used by Babylonians, Greeks, and Arabs for problem-solving and divining direction for millennia.[31] An upward pointing arrow is symbolic of shooting

---

[30] Protas, Brown, Smith, & Jaffe 2001

[31] "Belomancy" n.d.

for a higher ideal. It speaks to the true goal-setting part of our nature; the fabric of our beings.

In my doodles I always had a vertical arrow pointing a little to the right to symbolize my journey up and to the right. The phrase, "up and to the right," in this context means to aspire to do the right. In other words, make things a little better in all areas and rise above your status quo. The arrow also gave me a sense of direction and hope in my recovery and to find a target as well.

The names of the four points of my compass didn't come until I studied Dr. Jordan Peterson's lecture series, "The Psychological Significance of The Biblical Stories."[32] I was now able to finalize my working compass by adding the words "Order" and "Chaos" to the ends of the vertical line to give it meaning.

> "**Order** is a place, situation or state where things are predictable; you're on solid ground and you know what will happen next. Too much order can become boring, restrictive or even repressive. Too little order and there's not enough structure. A balance allows you to relax and feel comfortable.
>
> **Chaos** is a state or place where things are unpredictable and uncertain. We don't know

---

[32] Peterson, 2017

what's going to happen next and that can make chaos thrilling. Chaos can also be destructive as well as creative. Too much chaos and you are overwhelmed, anxious and afraid."[33]

Every day we must try to move our life from Chaos to Order in whatever small way we can. The up and to the right arrow represents my aim to bring Order out of Chaos.

God only knows what will happen to us if we put our house in order. An ancient king speaking to his people said, "See that all things are done in wisdom and order for it is not requisite that a man should run faster than he has strength."[34] There were many times when I found myself trying to run faster than I had strength. I would stumble or fall causing personal anxiety, chaos and failure.

Chaos comes to our lives in many different ways. My mind turned to an incident recorded in my journal on Monday, June 9, 2008, about a year into my rehab. "The doctor called with the results of my biopsy, it is cancer. I need surgery. It's malignant melanoma. The doctor is scheduling surgery this Thursday!" My mind went everywhere all at once: mortality, family history of cancer, what about rehab and so on.

The old serpent, named Chaos, will show up many times and in many ways in our lives. Chaos is a catalog of life's experiences: betrayal, accidents, abuse, and loss to

---

[33] Peterson, 2017

[34] Mosiah 4:27

name a few. Looking at my compass, and specifically my upward arrow, helps me find clarity of mind and see that I can make improvements, even if only a little and that brings peace and comfort to me.

An arrow shot straight up does not make any forward progress. I remember a time when my uncle took me out in the front yard of the family farm. He had a powerful hunting bow and he shot an arrow straight up into the air. It went completely out of sight. At that point both he and I were terrified! We had no idea where the arrow was going to come down. We hid under the eaves of the house and waited for what seemed like an eternity until the arrow made its atmospheric re-entry and sunk deep into the grass just a few feet away!

Shooting an arrow straight up wastes the applied energy and there is little advancement in any direction. There is much to be said for a planned trajectory or going up and a few degrees to the right or aiming at a target. I put the arrow on my compass about 20° to the right as a constant reminder to "go up and to the right."

Colors

My compass model started with a green circle. I chose that color because green symbolizes life, safety and harmony.[35] As a boy in Canada, I was taught the eternal nature of the evergreen trees and how almost every

---

[35] "Color Wheel Pro" n.d.

continent has an evergreen of some kind. I even wore a little plastic evergreen tree around my neck.

On my compass, I stayed true to the original four colors of the indigenous people's medicine wheel as found in the reports of the Museum of Ontario Archaeology. The color white is on top or north and represents a clean, pure mind. Yellow is to the right or east representing the spirit and light. The bottom or south is red representing heart and emotion. Finally, to the left or west is black; representing our physical body that returns to the earth.[36]

The Lines

Taking what I had learned from the scriptures and the ancients, I divided the green circle into four distinct quarters or quadrants. These represent the elements of my life that I have influence over. These four areas give us clarity and something that we can improve upon. I can strengthen myself and hold myself accountable!

The crossed lines in the Compass Model are rich in symbols in many philosophies, civilizations, and religious traditions.

The vertical line suggests to the mind a path from Chaos to Order or from earth to heaven and into the realm of spirits. It shows the true, dual nature of man, both the spiritual and the temporal. This upward trajectory indicates the constant tension between Order and Chaos in our lives.

---

[36] Genesis 3:19 KJV

It is a call to lift ourselves out of chaos and try to bring order in each of the four quadrants.

I have learned that by being truly honest with myself, I can cultivate more order in my thinking, in my spirit, in my emotional and physical development. I can do better.

This center vertical line says to me, "If I can look up, I can get up!" Some days in my recovery it took all that I had just to look up; literally to raise my gaze and to look steady and upward, and that was enough!

The arrow, up and to the right, gives me the hope and the desire to choose to avoid Chaos. I even like the way I feel when I say, "I am moving up and to the right!"

The horizontal line represents the many horizons we will see in our life on earth. Our journey here is a decision-making process, from beginning to end. Do we say yes or no? Do we go left or right? Do we rise up or fall down? There are countless decisions we must make daily; second by second and moment to moment.

The horizontal line is a reminder that all decisions are ours to make. Practically every choice falls somewhere between Good and Evil. With my Christian background it was easy for me to add the titles "Good" and "Evil." I think of this line as my personal responsibility line.

The labels "Good" and "Evil" may seem too extreme for some. This was the case when my Compass Model was examined at a branding seminar in Scottsdale, Arizona. The horizontal line titles were challenged by an expert as being too harsh. One of the participants called my home office in

Chapter Five

Dallas during the seminar and they wondered if I would consider changing the names. The group offered up softer words like "Workable and Unworkable" or "Functional and Nonfunctional" as possible alternatives.

On the speaker phone, I offered my quick and unflinching opinion, "No! Good and Evil are universal struggles." I truly believe that all of our daily decisions, to one degree or another, boil down to those two categories: Good or Evil. I know that may sound too black and white to some; however when we are in crisis and all looks bleak and gray, a little black and white thinking can be helpful. Life is a constant decision-making process.

In my early recovery days I was on what I called my "15 second clock." I had to decide every 15 seconds to see if I could make it another 15 seconds without giving up and going back to drugs and into relapse. I picked a time frame that I thought I could go without using drugs. In the world of cognitive behavior this technique is called, "The Framing Effect." This continued for weeks and was exhausting. Slowly I could go from 15 seconds to 30 seconds to 1 minute. This may sound manic yet at that point my recovery was manic. I had gone for years not making good choices and now I was paying the price to teach my brain how to make better decisions. Repetition is the mother of learning and it sucks!

You may have some trauma, drama, or unwanted behaviors that you want to remove from your life. What decision can you make right now that would improve your situation? What can you do to move toward the "Good" end of the spectrum? Can you reframe the problem using a positive decision and then reinforce it when it starts to go negatively? Repeat this until only positive decisions remains.

My sobriety was very tenuous. At any point I could've made the fatal decision to give up. I learned that you can make more good decisions in 15 seconds than you can imagine.

The Good and Evil line reminds me that all the decisions are mine to make. I think **C.S.** Lewis said it best: "There is no neutral ground in the universe. Every square inch, every split second is claimed by God, (Order) and counterclaimed by Satan (Chaos)." I believe it is my duty to observe my situation as honestly as I can and then move my thoughts, words and deeds toward the Good. We are not looking for perfection. We are just looking for progress in each of the four quadrants.

Finally, in **the center of my compass,** I put a small, white dot. It may sound silly, but I love this dot. It is the point or the meaning of Living One Life. It focuses my goal to balance my mind, spirit, emotions, and body. The center dot on the cross creates an intense feeling of alignment. It reminds me to be prepared and engaged in my life.

My Live One Life Compass is a pointer and a guide for me in my recovery! It has been time-tested by my clients and it improves lives no matter the trauma, drama, or addictive behaviors you want to change! Remember, the unconscious mind is listening for instructions. It is our responsibility to give the subconscious what it needs.

Chapter Five

The Relationship Alignment Model and the Compass Model are tools that we can use to focus on Living One Life.

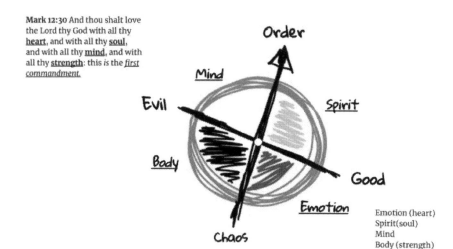

Mark 12:30 And thou shalt love the Lord thy God with all thy **heart**, and with all thy **soul**, and with all thy **mind**, and with all thy **strength**: this is the *first commandment.*

Emotion (heart)
Spirit(soul)
Mind
Body (strength)

I have learned to use these models to monitor and nurture my mind, spirit, emotions, and physical fitness so that I could live a drug-free, drama-free life. When trauma came, I recovered more quickly. As I explored this new territory of being truthful to myself and to others, I found my life having more wisdom and meaning. As I went through group therapy I realized that careful, truthful, articulated speech transformed Order out of Chaos.

I was neck-deep in rehab and recovery. I was using two Twelve Step Programs: the "Just for Today Daily Meditations for Recovering Addicts," put out by Narcotics Anonymous[37] and the "Addiction Recovery Program: A Guide

---

[37] Narcotics Anonymous World Services, 1992

to Addiction Recovery and Healing"[38] of the **LDS** Family Services. **S**ome of it made sense and resonated with me while other concepts seemed like they were from outer space.

I had read or listened to a good portion of the *Harvard Classics*, as well as *Seven Habits of Highly Effective People, Man's Search for Meaning, See You at The Top, How to Win Friends and Influence People and The Holy Scriptures.* I had gotten an extensive education through my new iPod library, yet I felt a real need to distill this information into basic elements that were easy for me to implement. I wanted wise, time-tested "calls to action" so that I could make quick course corrections in my recovery and that would not overwhelm me.

---

[38] LDS Family Services, 2005

With the compass as my centerpiece, I drew another circle around it and extended the vertical and horizontal lines to give me four more blank quadrants that I could fill in. I developed simple, two-word commands that I could look at multiple times a day to help stimulate and maintain balance and sanity.

Command Circle

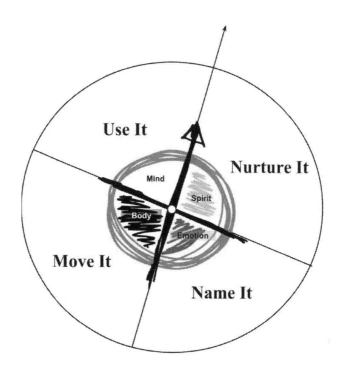

It is my hope that you won't minimize them due to their simplicity. Just as with many important things in life, they are simple to say yet another thing to do. Kind of like saying, "I'll keep my room clean," or "I'll always do my homework first," or "I will lose a few pounds." These are easy things to say yet rarely easy to do, especially in the beginning, and that's where I was.

Don't be put off by the word "command." I could've used suggestion, instruction, precept, or wish. I only want you to understand and win!

I believe you have a reverent responsibility and stewardship to develop yourself in each of the individual quadrants.

Honesty

This is the first step. We need to be brutally honest as we engage in each of the quadrants. Normally we tend to deny the seriousness of our behaviors or we minimize the impact of our actions on ourselves and others. I wasted so much time manufacturing stories (lying) and trying to blame other people for my situations. I went to great lengths and expended a lot of energy to avoid admitting I was wrong. The truth is, over time, people really don't care if we declare our mistakes but they will forever remember if we lie or deceive them! This principle is very powerful and even applies to us when we deceive ourselves.

I was amazed at how much simpler life got when I admitted I was wrong. The world didn't end and I didn't have to hide in shame. I had been so hard on myself for a long time yet I found that the sooner I admitted my mistakes; the sooner I could deal with them and move on.

Changing your mind might seem like an obscure form of honesty still you have to if you want to entertain new thoughts. Be willing to change and that includes your mind.

In this book, as in life, we are not looking for quick fixes; we are looking for a sustainable means of change. I would like to introduce you to my 3 Ps of Recovery: Patience, Progress & Persistence.

Patience

It's not easy to be patient with ourselves and others. We live in a world where, "I want it and I want it now!" is considered acceptable. Well it's not! It's unrealistic! We all need help being patient. I know early on in my rehab when facilitators and other addicts would say, "Take it one day at a time," I would almost throw a fit. Now I have come to understand that patience is "the suffering of afflictions, pain, toil, calamity...with a calm, unruffled temper."[39] Patience is being in the moment and enduring it without murmuring. It is the foundation of a strong character.

Progress

We must each measure progress in our own way. If we are doing a little better today than we did yesterday, then

---

[39] Webster's American Dictionary, 1828

that is sufficient. Comparing ourselves to others is fruitless and delays progress. A much better exercise is to compare ourselves to whom we were yesterday and evaluate this progress. Learning to be kind and gentle as we measure and honor our own little steps will serve us well.

Persistence

This trait is similar to the others in that it can be learned. Persistence is a self-mastery skill that we can all acquire. Developing the ability to be persistent can serve you in all aspects of your recovery.

"Nothing in this world can take the place of persistence. Talent will not; nothing is more common than unsuccessful men with talent. Genius will not; unrewarded genius is almost a proverb. Education will not; the world is full of educated derelicts. Persistence and determination alone are omnipotent. The slogan, 'Press On!' has solved and always will solve the problems of the human race."
— Calvin Coolidge

In my practice, many of my clients see perfection as the goal. I try to help them see that the 3 Ps: Patience, Progress & Persistence are far more attainable and are less overwhelming.

Chapter Six
Mind Quadrant

Neuroplasticity is just a fancy way of saying you can change your mind.   Dr. David W. Patterson

For thousands of years the quadrants of the medicine wheel had its own colors and symbols that depicted the knowledge of the universe. The color white embodies a clean and pure place. The herb sweetgrass is also known as "Holy Grass."[40]   These simple symbols, like parables, are rich in meaning, easy to remember and can impart great significance to those who are earnestly looking.

Our mind is the master control center. Every thought, feeling, and process in our body start with the brain. It is the seat of judgment, grace, and mercy in our inner world and will determine our decisions. "All that a man achieves and all that he fails to achieve is the direct result of his own thoughts."[41]

---

[40] Botanical Society of Britain and Ireland

[41] Allen, n.d., p. 8 – 9, 34

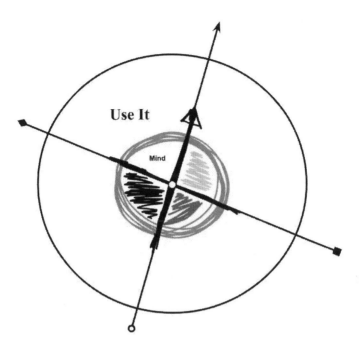

Use It

I know, "Use It" sounds way too simple. Well, it's supposed to be. These two-word commands should be easy because they need to be heard and understood quickly in the heat of life's battles. "Use It" instructs our minds and disrupts our current thinking. It encourages mental activity that stretches us intellectually. When we are in crisis with some type of trauma, drama or relapse, it is necessary to think fast and move in a healthy direction.

While recovering from my addiction, I needed a system that worked quickly for me. All I had to do was look at the compass, determine which of the four quadrants I was weakest in at the moment then apply the two-word command.

Chapter Six

So let's say my thinking wasn't good. Maybe it was disorganized. Possibly my thoughts were growing dark, anxious, or chaos or depression were sneaking in. I would look at my compass and decide it was the mind quadrant that I needed to work on. After all, I felt that my thinking wasn't right!

The first clue was the mind quadrant color. It was white, reminding me to keep my thoughts clean and pure. Then I would say aloud the simple command, "Use It." Many times this was enough to disrupt a negative thought-spiral. By just saying that simple reset phrase, "Use It," I could generally slow down enough to start to really investigate my concerns. Using my brain, I asked myself, "How did I start down this thought pattern?" or "What ideas are driving this depression?" Looking at the compass gave me a chance to invite the troublesome feelings to leave. With practice, I was able to escort unwanted concepts right out of my thinking entirely.

When teaching clients the proper way to use my compass, I ask them a question about their thinking. Their answer might be, "I don't know." At this point, I may ask, "Well let's ask your brain to figure it out!" Most times they are taken aback or offended. Once they recover from the question they start to come up with what they are really thinking instead of going to that automatic negative thought "I don't know."

It is extremely important to be able to articulate concepts and use your brain better. Just a quick command will jump-start your thinking. "Use It" improves your thought pattern instantly. Try this experiment. Think of something. Now use your mind to apply a little charity regarding your idea. Be kind to yourself. Is the feeling different now? Try the "Use It" technique often. The more you practice, the faster you will be able to improve.

Be frugal with your thinking. People say, "You must think I am..." They take on the task of thinking for you. This is an impossible job because they have no idea what you're imagining. In the next sentence they state, "My wife thinks I am..." Now they are reading their wife's mind. That same person will reason, "My boss thinks I am..." They assign themselves to think for their boss. Trying to feel for other people is an anxious way to live. Projecting your thoughts onto other people is exhausting and unproductive. Think your own thoughts and reason them well.

Mind Options

Read, Write, Ponder

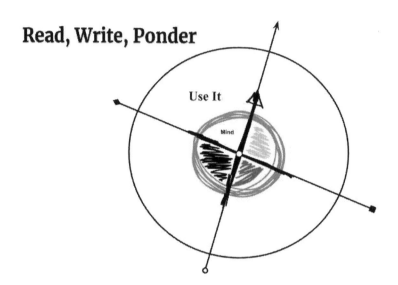

The options in the Mind quadrant consist of three simple action words to help improve your thinking. They are: Read, Write and Ponder. These are low-tech, no cost, and minimally invasive tools that will serve you well as you attempt DIY brain surgery.

OK, brain surgery might be a little strong, although re-structuring your thinking is not. I know it may sound funny to hear reading prescribed by one who is dyslexic and has attention issues. I'm not alone. Both the scientific and academic experts agree that you can improve your mind by developing these three reliable habits.

Read

When I say reading I don't just mean the written word. There are many sources and ways to take in quality content. The most low-tech, never-fail-miracle is a real book but there are digital options available including both audio and video.

"Reading is one of the best ways to structure your mind. Take the time to read from the best books."[42] Reading raises your intelligence. Studies show an increase in vocabulary which improves communication. With better communication skills you can verbalize your thoughts and feelings more accurately in your social circles. Reading well-written novels, autobiographies, etc. increases empathy towards others. By reading about people's emotions and feelings you can develop your own emotional reference library[43].

For me, with my dyslexia, a paper or digital book is a very slow go. I found that audiobooks are much faster although that speed comes at a price: my ability to retain the information! I like the combination of following the text in a book/device while listening to the audio. This is the most beneficial for me. It took a very long time to set my pride and ego aside and do whatever it took to read. Decide if and how you will improve your mind. Sadly 30% of us don't even read 1 book in a year. "The man who does not read

---

[42] Berns, Blaine, Prietula, & Pye 2013

[43] Kidd & Castano, 2013

good books has no advantage over the man who can't read them."[44]

Write

Unfortunately writing in a journal is not common in our average day-to-day life. Less than 15% of adults keep a daily diary. Journaling, whether it's in leather Moleskine or on a computer screen, has enormous benefits for our mental and physical health. It really doesn't matter what you write.

The exercise of getting your thoughts out of your head and putting them on paper is a great start. It gives you the opportunity to evaluate your feelings, maybe for the first time. Just 10 to 15 minutes of journal writing every few days will bring calming and healing effects.[45] My own recovery journal was hit or miss. I only wrote when I needed to. I found it helped me process difficult events and compose a coherent narrative about my experiences. You too can process negative emotions associated with traumatic memories of your life in your own words. These will be far more personal and helpful.

I had to overcome a lot of self-imposed rules that held me back from journaling for many years. I believed that my spelling needed to be correct. It does not! I believed that all the grammar must be correct. It does not! For some strange and grandiose reason I thought I was writing for

---

[44] 1910 July, The Southern Workman, Volume 39, Number 7, Comment by Joseph D. Eggleston, Jr.

[45] Blakie & Wilhelm, 2005

future generations. I am not! I had to come to the realization that I was just writing for me. I had to give myself permission to let go and do my best to write with integrity and just write the truth.

If you are a techniques kind of person, The Center for Journal Therapy has a great website that can help with "14 Writing Techniques for Your Journal."[46]

After developing my compass, I used the journal option to help clear my head of toxic thinking and unrealistic expectations. It makes a difference when you see your ideas out in front of you.

The benefits include long-term improvements in mood, stress, and depression. Not only does writing make you less likely to get sick, it speeds up healing and increases the chances of fighting diseases.[47] Journaling is one of my overarching principles that positively serve all four quadrants of the compass.

Your journal is your safe place. Keep it safe. Keep it private. It's for your eyes only. Not for your spouse, family, friends, or even a therapist to read, of course you can discuss your experiences with any of them!

Ponder

Most of us will have a hard time defining what pondering means. Let's turn to Mr. Webster: "To weigh in the mind; to consider and compare the circumstances or

---

[46] Adams n.d.

[47] Rodriguez, 2013

Chapter Six

consequences of an event, or the importance of the reasons for or against a decision."[48]

Pondering is what you use to filter and adjust to the current events of your life. The act of weighing out your options in a particular situation is what can moderate the decisions you make. It is one of the tools that helps you process the content you consume and adapt it to your needs. It is thinking your thoughts for yourself. I have learned that slowing down and pondering can really make a difference in how I perceive the world around me. Learning to become the gatekeeper of our mind must include pondering.

One of my greatest fears as I worked my way through my rehab was that I may have permanently damaged my brain and therefore my ability to think. I remembered how I wore my counselors out by asking them how much damage that particular drug had done to my brain and if it would ever come back. Would I ever be the same? Their answer brought me no solace. "We don't know!" Looking back at it now I realize I didn't want to be the same. I wanted to change. Everything! After all, that's what rehab was all about.

I researched and I couldn't find any good answers to my fearful question. Fact: "The human brain is immensely complex, containing more connections than there are stars in the Milky Way galaxy. Scientists have a better handle on our vast universe than on the three-pound organ inside a human's head."[49]

---

[48] Webster, 1828

[49] World Science Festival, 2006

The mind's complexities are truly beyond our ability to understand. What we do know is that the mind and body are subject to the same, great, universal, and natural laws of life. Primarily, we reap what we sow or in modern, computer terms: garbage in, garbage out.

This also applies to the human mind.[50] As we sow new ideas, it is important that our heart is ready to receive them. What we feed our minds will determine its capacity to process and cope with the many joys and pains of our life. It is our divine responsibility to supply ourselves with the highest quality of stimulating content. We need that raw ability to think on our own behalf so that we can successfully navigate the world around us. We may not understand all the complexities of our brain however we do have a great deal of control and influence over this miraculous structure.

Speaking of the mind, I want to discuss the concept of filtering our thoughts. Keeping them clean and pure is not easy. In this day and age of devices and internet, it is tempting to give our minds over to other sophisticated sources. The color white in the mind quadrant is there to remind us to control what enters in. I have found that by choosing to filter my personal content I can make any situation better.

Scientific and anecdotal research[51]confirms that if we will approach any subject or activity with a good attitude,

---

[50] GIGO Washington Post, 1987

[51] Hill, Allemand, & Roberts, 2014

gratitude, and enthusiasm, we will be much more productive and successful at whatever we strive to do![52]

I wish I could say that I used these three adjusting filters; however, it wasn't until I was in rehab that I did a good self-analysis of my thinking. What I learned was that I am like many people and prone to ignore these attributes.

My experience has taught me that attitude, gratitude, and enthusiasm can be contagious. I remember once in a Narcotics Anonymous (NA) meeting, a man came in. I'll call him Jim. He was dirty, smelly and disheveled. I was still in my own self-centered space, sitting there passing judgment on him. I thought, "Geez man could you at least have a shower and comb your hair before coming to the meeting!"

The facilitators of the meeting and some of the participants were excited and grateful that Jim was there. Millions of men and women who need help never take the daunting step to attend a meeting. I didn't share their enthusiasm. I remember spending most of that meeting smelling and judging Jim. I had never seen him before and I didn't know his back-story. Somehow, I got some sense of feeling good about myself through judging him, a little self-righteous chemical dump.

Over the weeks I got to know him and the troubles that he suffered. I also saw what the attitude, gratitude, and enthusiasm of the facilitators and other group members were doing to help Jim put himself together. With a little praise and attention and significant work by Jim, he could

---

[52] Wooden & Carty, 2009

motivate himself to make the best of his sad and difficult situation. Getting up, cleaning up, and making it to a meeting was huge! He was participating and caring for himself. Slowly, month after month, he was putting his life back together and not lying on the floor in his shabby, little room waiting for someone to rescue him.

What I noticed about Jim and myself was that we both had our own problems: he started off dirty and smelly and I started off arrogant and judgmental. I could see the progress in Jim although I wasn't so sure about myself. What I was learning though was that if I would give myself the chance and adjust my attitude and enthusiasm I could be grateful for and improve any situation.

The dirty, little, dark spot in my mind that caused me to judge Jim was now becoming cleaner and clearer. My thinking was becoming more pure and charitable toward him. I found myself looking inward and in so doing I found that I respected Jim. I was grateful for what he had taught me.

ANT

Automatic

Negative

Thoughts

Automatic negative thoughts for many of us are our natural default mode. Finding fault is as easy as rolling off a log. I have found this to be true in my life. We also find that these destructive, automatic negative thoughts are easy to conjure up and lob at our friends and family. Once in use, we get our little feel-good chemical dump and continue to recycle them repeatedly.

To defeat the ANTs, we must first be aware of them. This self-examination is not easy. It can cause discomfort, however we should push through it. We need to use our mind to understand our mind. By filtering our thoughts through the concepts of attitude, gratitude and enthusiasm our mind becomes purer and cleaner as symbolized by the white color on the compass.

We must change the way we perceive situations and people. If you are anything like me and are quick to judge, this is a difficult thing to do. You might employ one of the tools above including gratitude to adjust this self-righteous way of thinking. As you do this your toxic attitude is dissipated and you can see more clearly

As I was refocusing during my recovery, I had to continually look at my compass colors, commands and options to chart a positive course. Even though they were mine, they were often foreign to me. It was a new way of thinking and a different path of taking responsibility for me.

By studying my compass, I could figure out whether it was my mind, spirit, emotions or body that was depleting my energy and start working on that particular quadrant. Many of us think we are taking care of ourselves however we usually treat ourselves far worse than we treat friends and family.

We all know our faults and we like to tell ourselves about them continually. In my case, I compounded them until it got so noisy in my head that I had to find a release or some form of peace. I tried to find it in drugs, alcohol, trauma, drama, and any other unhealthy distraction. My subconscious was waiting for directions to start a chemical cocktail.

I fed negative thoughts into my brain and my brain believed them. Here is an example of my negative feedback loop: "I am a troublesome youth and that caused my dad enough pain to shoot himself. He is dead and I killed him." That was my extreme story and it continued to play in the background every waking hour and almost every night.

I wished for things to be different by using "if only thinking."[53] If only I had done...if only I could...or if only they had... This was a very exhausting way to live, constantly reliving the same past traumatic event over and over again.

Chaotic or Negative Thinking

1. **All-or-Nothing Thinking:** "I have to do things perfectly and anything less is a failure."
2. **Focusing on the Negatives:** "Nothing goes my way. It feels like one disappointment after another."
3. **Negative Self-Labeling:** "I'm a failure. If people knew the real me, they wouldn't like me. I am flawed."
4. **Catastrophizing:** "If something is going to happen, it'll probably be the worst-case scenario."[54]

---

[53] Covey, 2013

[54] Melemis, 2010

The Lesson of the Tally Counter

One day during a group session they suggested that we put a rubber band around our wrist and every time we had a negative thought we were to snap the rubber band. Of course, I asked for clarification. "Is a negative thought about myself, others or the weather?" Any negative thought was the answer. I put on the rubber band and snapped it immediately because the rebel in me said, "This is stupid." SNAP. "I'm not doing this." SNAP. "Pain is not a good motivator; whoever thought this up was an idiot." SNAP. This rubber band snapping was not working for me and I quit.

A few weeks went by and we were having another conversation about negative thoughts. This time it was proposed that we get a tally counter to count how many negative thoughts we were having. A tally counter is a small device that someone will hold in their hand to keep track of scores or people in a crowd. Every time you click, it adds another number to the count.

This exercise involved numbers, which always interested me, so I thought I would try this technique to check out my negative thinking. There was a Big Five Sporting Goods store near the bus stop so after my day at rehab, I went in. Even though money was tight, I spent $6 and bought a tally counter.

I thought I could use the time on the bus to see how many negative thoughts I had on my way home. Remember, this is a 90-minute bus, train, and then bus commute. I got on the bus and I clicked the clicker every time I judged somebody, myself or thought something was stupid. I clicked it for every negative thought that entered my brain. I did not look at the counter. I wanted to know how many negative thoughts I would have on my way home. For some reason, I got very committed to this experiment!

Now I want you to know I did not increase my internal complaining for this test. I just tried to go at my regular rate of negativity. When I got off the bus 90 minutes later and looked at the tally counter I was stunned! 272 negative thoughts in a single commute! I walked into the house and got out the calculator. 272 ÷ 90 = 3.02. Three negative thoughts per minute! I just sat there thinking, "I'm doing this to myself. Nobody is doing this to me!"

After a period of pondering this, I went back to the calculator. Let's say I'm awake 16 hours a day; that's 960 minutes. If my bus experiment was accurate, and I felt it was, then that's 2,899 negative, fault finding, or complaining thoughts a day. That's 1,058,932 negative or judging thoughts a year! I was 52 years old and I had been this way for as long as I could remember, so let's call it 50 years: 52,946,640! This number literally brought me to tears and it does again as I write this down. I had undermined myself with almost fifty-three million negative and crippling thoughts in my lifetime. No wonder I needed drugs to make myself feel better!

A side note: I shared this story with a Life Coach colleague of mine, Lori Beard,[55] and she now gives a tally

---

[55] Beard, 2018

counter to each of her clients when it comes time to examine their thinking. I suggest this exercise to all who are willing to change the way they think. Are you ready to exterminate those self-destructive automatic negative thoughts, or ANTs? Are you willing to improve your self-talk?

After the bus experiment, my little arrow that points up and to the right on the compass became a genuine emotional symbol for me. Looking at the arrow gave me hope; hope that I could do better with my thinking. We all suffer from what Zig Ziglar called, "stinking thinking,"[56] and we are the only ones that can stop this internal fermentation.

On the compass model, the white, mind quadrant is in the center. In the outer circle is the command, "Use It." Continue moving outward to find the Option Words, "Read, Write, and Ponder."

---

[56] Ziglar, 2000

Read, Write, Ponder

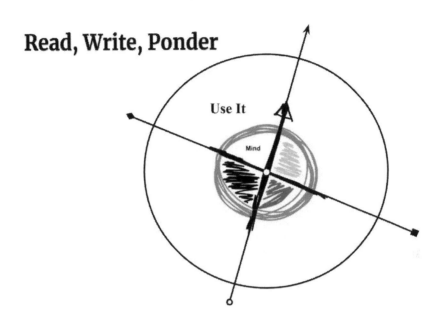

Tony Buzan first introduced mind mapping to the world. It is now a tool used by academics, students, business professionals and many other individuals to manage, organize and reimagine information in a new and highly structured way.[57] On the following page I have given you a sample of a simple mind map for the word "Write."

---

[57] iMindMap, 2015

Sample Mind Map for Write

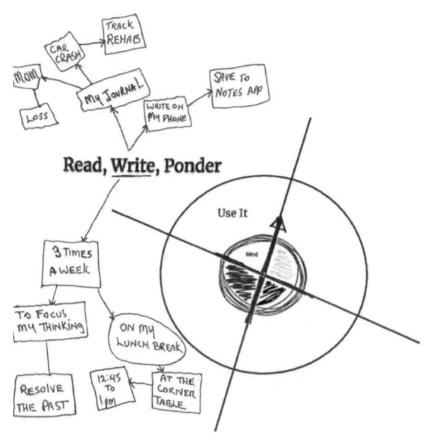

The Mind Mapping space is all the blank area surrounding the compass. Write all you can think of for each of the words in the Options area. I'm sure you can completely fill the page as you empty your brain on each of these Option Words!

Now let's look at the most powerful tool of them all; the "Actions Page."

The 5Ws or Actions Page

The 5Ws is provided for you to personalize your compass! This worksheet is where you will answer the 5Ws questions: Who, What, Where, When, and Why. These simple questions help with your basic problem solving and goal setting.

Here's how it works! In this example, the "Who" is you. Let's say you chose "Write" from the three Option Words. Underline that word. Next take your time to answer this particular word like:

- ❀ What shall I write

- ❀ Where shall I write

- ❀ When shall I write

- ❀ Why shall I write

In each chapter you will be given worksheets. Mind map the options for each quadrant. Answer the 5Ws questions. In the Mind quadrant, the options are Read, Write and Ponder.

Read Mind Map

Read, Write, Ponder

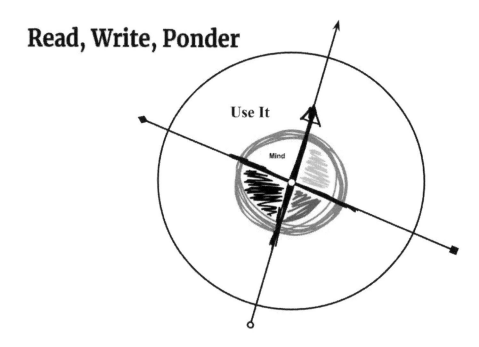

Read 5Ws

Who? Me

What will I read?

_____

_____

_____

Where will I read? (What devices?)

_____

_____

_____

When will I read?

_____

_____

_____

Why am I reading?

_____

_____

_____

Write Mind Map

Read, Write, Ponder

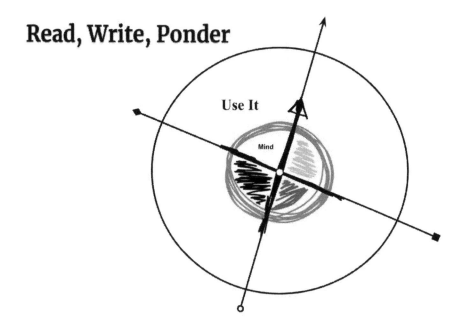

Write 5Ws

Who? Me

What will I write?

_____

_____

_____

Where will I write? (What devices?)

_____

_____

_____

When will I write?

_____

_____

_____

Why am I writing?

_____

_____

_____

Ponder Mind Map

Read, Write, Ponder

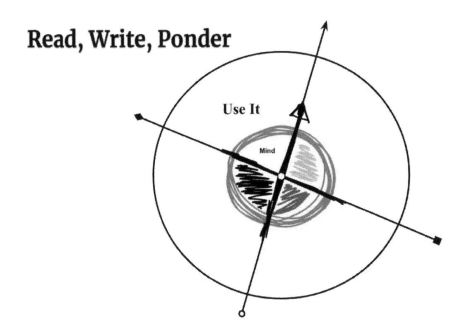

Ponder 5Ws

Who? Me

What will I ponder?

_____

_____

_____

Where will I ponder? (What devices?)

_____

_____

_____

When will I ponder?

_____

_____

_____

Why am I pondering?

_____

_____

_____

Powerful Overarching Practices

There are very powerful practices that you can employ that will impact your growth in all four quadrants of your compass. They are journaling, meditation and smiling.

Journaling

I have found that even intermittent, sketchy attempts at journal keeping have been very beneficial to my self-evaluation. Many of my current, daily practices stemmed from notes in my journal. Most of the anecdotes in this book came from my weak, inconsistent note taking. Much can be reaped from where very little was sown.

Now before you get all dismissive, thinking this is just hyperbole or that these activities are too touchy-feely for you, let's see what the experts are saying:

"If you are suffering in the aftermath of a traumatic event, journaling can help you find the good in life. It can even help you see the positive side of experiencing the trauma, which helps reduce the severe symptoms that can accompany trauma."[58]

"In general, people diagnosed with Major Depressive Disorder reported significantly lower depression scores after three days of expressive writing, 20 minutes per day."[59]

---

[58] Ullrich & Lutgendorf, 2002

[59] Krpan, Kross, Berman, Deldin, Askren, & Jonides, 2013

Meditation

The second practice that will assist you in mastering all the quadrants is meditation. At the beginning of my recovery, I vehemently pushed back at the mention of meditation. I now know, at that time, I was afraid to be alone with my thoughts. It takes great courage to sit and listen to your inner voice!

I needed help getting started. At Kaiser Rehab, we had facilitators who would read to us out of guided meditation books for about 10-15 minutes, 2 times a week. Today, my meditation usually takes place early in the morning before or after personal prayer. After my morning yoga, my meditation resembles the stereotypical monk sitting cross-legged. I had to give myself permission to sit quietly on my living room floor and listen to my brain and try to get it to be still. Please don't be afraid of sitting with your thoughts. I know it sounds counterintuitive to reduce your thinking to improve your thinking, yet it is so true.

YouTube is a great resource to find assistance with your meditation practices. There are many that are made up of sound or music only. These make a good background for study, relaxation, or sleep; however there is power in the spoken word especially when you are getting started. I can recommend the Australian, Jason Stephenson, on YouTube. I particularly like his video "Spoken Meditation for Addiction: Help for Substance, Gambling, Alcohol, Drugs, and Depression."[60] It has been watched over 200,000 times. Jason

---

[60] Jason Stephenson – Sleep Meditation Music, 2016

currently has over 1,000,000 subscribers for all of his videos. It's ok if you don't like this one; please keep searching for other assisted meditation or guided imagery videos.

I know it is hard to set your biases aside long enough to help yourself. Be kind and brave in your own behalf and push through. Take time to write in your journal and meditate. I've said it before and I will continue to say it: there is no one else coming to do this work for you and it's work that must be done.

Smile

The practice of smiling was introduced early on in rehab. We were to hold a mirror in front of our face and smile. A lot of us in the group session could not even look in the mirror. The self-loathing was too much, even for me. I was not a fan of this exercise and thought it was a bunch of B.S. All my life I had a "resting angry face." When I sat relaxed, my face just naturally looked angry, or at best, neutral. Looking back on it now, I feel bad for the therapist. It must've been like giving a cat a bath to get me to participate. Eventually I brought the mirror up and cracked an artificial smile.

Over the coming weeks we practiced, with and without the mirror. We also held a pencil between our teeth to turn up the corners of our mouth and create a smile and I became a believer.

Smiling will:

- Change your mood

- Relieve stress

- Boost your immune system

- Lower your blood pressure

- Release endorphins and serotonin

Smiling has become one of the main tools in my daily tool belt. Whenever I walk past a mirror I say, "David, smile; you're worth the effort," and immediately I feel better.

Smiling is an act of service. When you smile at others, they smile back and everyone feels uplifted. Please try to muster up the courage to smile many times a day, for yourself and those around you!

Chapter Seven
Spirit and Light

Spirit is in the upper right quadrant of the compass. Yellow represents light, knowledge and the morning sun. This easterly quarter portrays a very delicate, sacred, fleeting element of our life: our spirituality! Notice that the divider between mind and spirit is the up and to the right arrow of hope. The apostle, Paul, tells us that hope is an anchor of the soul, both sure and steadfast.[61] Without hope, all is lost. Thus, spirituality is a part of our life, our inner, divine nature or spark.

I particularly like the color yellow as it is reminiscent of warm candlelight. It reminds me of my own divine light in this world. We dramatically underestimate the power of just one little candle. As a Scoutmaster, I would ask the boys who were sitting around the campfire, how far away they thought you could see a single candle? Some of them guessed 100 feet; some said a quarter-mile, while others

---

[61] Hebrew 6:19 KJV

thought maybe even a mile. The truth is that a single candle on a dark night can be seen some 10 miles away. Another study took the curvature of the earth out of the equation and reports a single candle can be seen as far as 30 miles away with the human eye.[62]

We all underestimate the power of one little candle. Or do we? Candle sales in the U.S. are roughly $2.3 billion a year.[63] It would seem that we are naturally drawn to the warm light of its glow.

Our personal light upon this world will be felt for generations. We may not think of it but the decisions our ancestors made have determined how and where we live. This is true for you. The decisions you make today will determine how your future generations will live. We all influence people and situations; whether it's for good or bad. Slow down and reflect on your spiritual quadrant and appreciate the light that you shine on others.

"Let your light shine before others, that they may see your good deeds and glorify your Father in heaven."[64] No one else is authorized to use your light; your spark of divinity. How you use it is your responsibility. No one can determine that for you, nor would you want them to. Do you feed or starve your personal light to this world?

In the spirit quadrant there is the two-word command, "Nurture It." Your source of spiritual strength is whatever

---

[62] Krisciunas, 2013

[63] White n.d.

[64] Matthew 5:16 NIV

Chapter Seven

you perceive it to be or possibly you are well-grounded and have great faith in one of the many spiritual traditions.

Nurture It

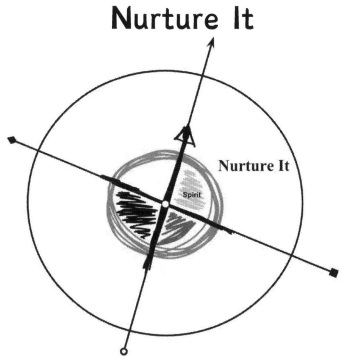

Many scientific and medical professionals have come to know the importance and need for spiritual balance. The renowned Cleveland Clinic has a "Center for Spiritual Care" that provides for the spiritual and holistic care of patients, families, visitors, and caregivers. Professionals are once again making effective use of religious/spiritual heritage and theological understanding, combined with behavioral sciences for the care of their clients/patients.

If you have any kind of spiritual scaffolding then you can "Nurture" your beliefs by studying the materials and teachings of your faith.

Perhaps you are still looking for pieces to your spiritual foundation. This can be a very daunting and exciting search. You have many options. You may choose to anchor yourself in the 7 Chakras, Crystals, Mother Earth, Father Sky, our Feminine and Masculine Nature, or Nature herself. Nearly 75 percent of the world's population claim one of the five most influential religions of the world: Buddhism, Christianity, Hinduism, Islam, and Judaism. Even these are splintered into a very dynamic number nearing 4,200 religions.[65] Unfortunately only about 30% of the membership is fully engaged in their choice of spirituality. As you can see, the charge to "Nurture It" can get very complicated, very quickly!

Please don't be turned off or overwhelmed with all this talk of religion. To Live One Life with purpose, simplify this discussion to a belief in a power greater than yourself. Some call this their "Higher Power."

A wise man, when asked, "Do you believe in God?" replied, "I don't know what you mean by God, but I try to live my life as though God exists." Put in simple terms, "I act as if God exists."[66] I cannot and will not try to make this decision for you. This is your journey and this is your choice. Take your time. Search with an open mind. Try not to judge too quickly or harshly. Follow that which brings out the best in you and when it stops bringing out your best; re-evaluate. Find that which will honor and resonate both in your head and in your heart.

---

[65] "World Religions, Religion Statistics, Geography Church Statistics" Retrieved 5 March 2015

[66] Bite-sized Philosophy, 2017

Spirit Options

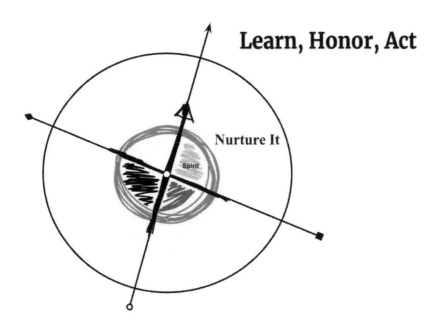

Learn, Honor, Act

The options in the Spirit quadrant consist of three simple one-word commands to help improve your spiritual strength and capacity. They are: "Learn, Honor, and Act." These three words will serve you well as you exercise them in your search to Live One Life. If you intend to come to some meaningful balance in your life; you will need some form of spiritual weight in the yellow quadrant of the compass.

Learn

What I mean by "learn" in this quadrant is learn what is important to you. Do you have a spiritual element to your life? Is there spiritual scaffolding that you can use to answer life's questions? Who am I? Where did I come from? What is the meaning of life? Where do I go when I die?

I am forever grateful to my parents who were willing to learn from those who were prepared to teach. Because of their open-mindedness to the Spirit and the Word, I have the scaffolding of my church to explore the big questions as well as build my faith and resolve. More importantly, I can hold fast to the iron rod of the God of my understanding.

If you have chosen the 7 Chakras, Buddhism, or Christianity, for example, as the framework that you will use to provide hope, meaning, purpose, and something to look forward to; learn about it! Search good books on your chosen belief. Study with those who already believe. Listen to their stories of how this path has served them well. Ask those of like minds, how their choice makes a difference in their daily decision-making. Ask if this style or doctrine is consistent with my own internal light or spirituality?

Think of your spiritual intake as you would the food that you eat or the water that you drink. You want it to be clean and pure and of good quality; after all, you plan on using this foundation to build your very best self. Your choice of what you believe must last throughout your life. In times of crisis, you can't have your inner light extinguished due to some external flood that overwhelms your faith.

"While traveling the path, you may experience many feelings of doubt, despair, fear, disappointment, and dislocation, as well as feelings of pleasure, joy, happiness and discovery. These are all important experiences and components to your search and will be displayed in the value system you will adapt to bring meaning to your existence."[67]

Constant learning and studying of what you believe strengthens you against the trauma, drama, and disasters that will befall you. None of us are immune to the hardships, tests, and adventures of this great journey. I have come to know, by experience, that spiritual things or things of the heart are not to be ignored because there are consequences. The prophet Muhammad said about spirituality, "Truly it is not their eyes that are blind, but their hearts."[68]

Honor

The church I belong to and the United States Marine Corps share this powerful charge: "Return with Honor." The Marine Corps' goal is to return from battle with honor and dignity. In my religion, it means return to God with honor, having done our very best in this life. As we learn and study our chosen spiritual path, the time will come when we start to embrace and feel the strength of our traditions. We will identify ourselves with that which we put our faith in. This is called honoring what we believe.

---

[67]"Six Dimensions of Wellness Model" by Bill Hettler, MD © National Wellness Institute, Inc.

[68]"The Pilgrimage" Quran 22:46

Chapter Seven

I once had a conversation with a woman at a lunch counter in a small town in Idaho. Somehow we got on the subject of religion. She made the statement that she was a "Jack Mormon." This is slang for a member of The Church of Jesus Christ of Latter-day Saints who doesn't live the principles of their religion. Knowing full well what a "Jack Mormon" was, I asked her, "Where do you meet?" She laughed and said, "No it's not a religion, it's just..." She thought for a moment, "I guess I'm not much for organized religion." I continued the quiz, "So you're more about 'disorganized' religion?" She laughed and said, "It seems that way!"

Many of us embrace different types, patterns, and rituals that make us feel better, however, beware of them becoming distractions and time-wasters. These habits and rituals might be considered "disorganized religions" in our lives.

Some of us dabble in traditions and religions yet aren't committed. We just go to a lazy, default position that seems to get us from day to day. The trouble with this is that it has no durability when trouble or tragedy strikes. If we are accustomed to doing the minimum in our spiritual quest, then we can only expect minimal recovery assistance when the tests of life come at us.

When I was in rehab, I attended yoga and meditation classes to find my spiritual center. I went begrudgingly at first, then to my surprise, over a matter of just a few weeks, subtle changes started to take place. I was more aware of my place in this world, who I was, and what I thought about myself.

Spirituality is a very personal and sacred part of my life. Through all the many tests and trials in recovery, trauma, and drama, I came to the knowledge that I must nurture my spirit. I also realized that I am responsible for my light and I need to respect the light of others.

In my recovery group many had hobbies, games or activities that were important to them, but relationships and traditions were at the heart of their family. Our spiritual lives are very personal and there is more to us than just emotions, body, mind, and the physical world around us.

Take a moment and write down rituals and traditions that are meaningful to you. Evaluate them and ask if they are serving you well spiritually.

_____

_____

_____

_____

_____

_____

_____

_____

_____

_____

_____

Do your beliefs and rituals cause you to look up and to the right? Is there hope in these rituals or do some of them fall flat? Or worse yet, do these things that you think of as your center or spiritual growth weaken you?

This is soul-searching work that requires a level of honesty and integrity that you may not be used to. Don't be fearful or think that some principle is too vague or even untouchable as you examine your spiritual life. "We fix our eyes not on what is seen, but on what is unseen, since what is seen is temporary, but what is unseen is eternal."[69]

I was raised in a church with a very structured lifestyle. Over the years I have run hot, cold and sometimes almost frozen in my faith. I have since defrosted and I am happily very active in church.

In the Bible, there is this verse, "The eye is the lamp of the body. If your eyes are healthy, your whole body will be full of light. If your eyes are unhealthy, your whole body will be full of darkness."[70] Remember, while putting yourself back together after traumatic experiences, everything is on the table for examination. You will need a light to show the way. If your light can't stand the scrutiny perhaps it's not for you.

A word of caution: During this evaluation you want to survive and thrive. Don't be like the surgeon that said, "The operation was a success, but the patient died." Be gentle

---

[69] 2 Cor. 4:18 NIV

[70] Matthew 6:22-23 NIV

with yourself; be kind and merciful yet relentless in your search.

Just like in the Mind quadrant, the Spirit quarter has a simple, circle command which is "Nurture It," meaning to nurture your spiritual self.

While working on my own recovery, I would look at or visualize my compass in times of distress. It would remind me that I have 4 areas in my life that I can influence. These simple, circle commands help flesh out ways to strengthen your spiritual life.

The first command is "Learn." Learn and study the traditions of your spiritual life. You owe it to yourself to embrace your faith. For those of you who are not involved with any organized religion, you still have spiritual needs.[71] For millennia spiritual beliefs and community have been there to assist through personal tragedy. Spirituality heals when life lessons are hard.

Everybody needs vital beliefs that give some sense of meaning and hope in the midst of losses, tragedies, and failures. We need to have values, priorities, and life commitments. These are usually centered on issues of justice, integrity, and love. These guide us personally and socially to live responsibly. "It is better to live each day in a way that is consistent with our values and beliefs than to feel untrue to ourselves."[72] Positive, meaningful values assist

---

[71] "Seven Spiritual Needs" n.d.

[72] Adapted from the National Wellness Institute (NWI)

us in times of recovery from traumatic and dramatic and addictive behaviors.

Act

There is a level of faith that produces good works, especially obedience, to the principles and commandments. As you study and learn about your chosen path, you will become adept at obeying the guiding principles. You are acting out what you believe. These activities will help you be happier, smarter, and more fulfilled in some meaningful way. True faith eliminates rationalization. It can lead to self-examination which can lead to change and growth.

"There is, however, a level of faith that not only governs our behavior but also empowers us to change what is and to make things happen that otherwise would not happen. I am speaking of faith not only as a principle of action but also as a principle of power."[73] This gives us great mental, physical, and emotional strength.

You may be active in your church or traditions. You may believe that you have great faith in your beliefs. "I don't care how much faith you have, I care about what sort of faithful actions you do. I believe you are braver than you know. I believe you have great power within you. So much life and so much to give to the world, but fear is the one

---

[73] Webb, 2017

thing standing in your way. Your desire to be safe and comfortable might be ruining your life."[74]

Acting on your honorable beliefs is the key to a meaningful life. If we adults are to recover from our life's traumas and dramas we must explore good, virtuous and mature beliefs. "When I was a child, I spoke and thought and reasoned as a child. When I grew up, I put away childish things."[75]

A quotation usually attributed to Shakespeare reads: "What e'er thou art, act well thy part." The "Old English" may not rest well on your ear, still the message is wise. Whatever you do; do it well!

The next few pages are yours to use to determine how you will seek out content for your Spirit quadrant. Map out your spiritual learning. Do your best to answer "Learn, Honor, and Act" using the 5Ws questions. Write down what you intend to study, where, when and why.

---

[74] Hour of Power "Faith is an Action" Oral Roberts http://hourofpower.org/faith-is-an-action/

[75] 1 Corinthians 13:11 NLT

Learn Mind Map

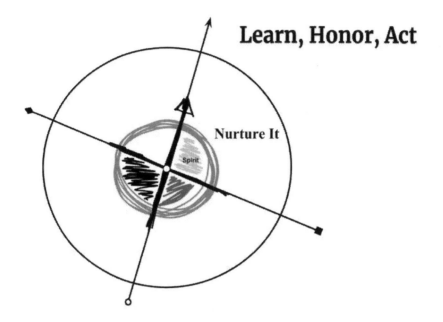

Learn, Honor, Act

Nurture It

Spirit

Learn 5Ws

Who?   Me

What will I learn?

_____

_____

_____

Where will I learn?

_____

_____

_____

When will I learn?

_____

_____

_____

Why am I learning?

_____

_____

_____

Honor Mind Map

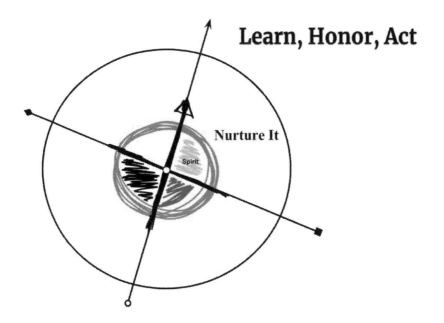

Learn, Honor, Act

Nurture It

Spirit

Honor 5Ws

Who?   Me

What do I honor?

_____

_____

_____

Where will I honor?

_____

_____

_____

When will I honor?

_____

_____

_____

Why am I honoring?

_____

_____

_____

Act Mind Map

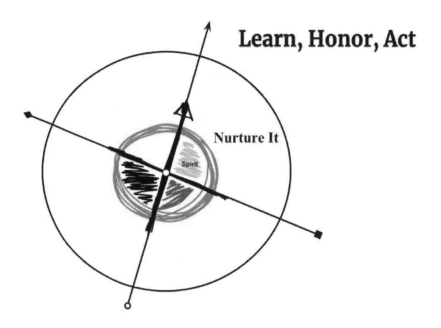

Act 5Ws

Who?   Me

What do I act?

_____

_____

_____

Where will I act?

_____

_____

_____

When will I act?

_____

_____

_____

Why am I acting?

_____

_____

_____

Chapter Eight
Faces of Emotions

"No one can make you feel inferior without your consent."
Eleanor Roosevelt

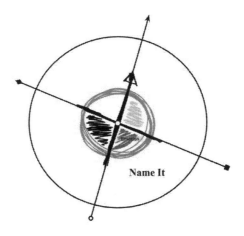

In the lower right of the compass is the red quadrant. In ancient, aboriginal medicine wheels, this quarter represented the direction south; the season of summer; the herb sage; and the element of emotion. This bottom quarter brings to my mind a fire in the belly; those deep-down emotions. We feel them and see their consequences in our lives. For too many of us, these emotions are an enigma; our own personal, untamed frontier to be explored and developed. For example, anger temporarily empowers us because the brain produces adrenaline and analgesic processes. This chemical dump temporarily relieves vulnerability and increases our confidence; fear and shame are disempowered.

If you can develop the skill of identifying your emotions, then you can observe and alter unwanted destructive, emotional patterns. If you, your coach, or a self-help book focuses on only one emotion, you may exaggerate its significance and not get the whole picture. You may feel like a victim; misunderstood by those around you. Your recovery will take a long time of unnecessary hard work during which you will notice little progress. The sooner you develop a rich, emotional vocabulary, the sooner you can come to terms with your feelings and their causes and effects.

To help you on the path is the simple, two-word command, "Name It." I developed "Name It" to help me focus on what I was really feeling. At this stage of my recovery, I wasn't all that interested in the source of my emotions. I just wanted to accurately name them. I was learning that there were more than three emotions and it was my job to discover them. Can you accurately name your emotions and feelings? By giving them names you get your power back. Awareness is essential to wellness. Once you have named them, you will be able to change these emotions based upon your own developed thoughts, philosophies, and behaviors.

There is good news and bad news. The good news is you are the one calling the shots. The bad news is you are the one calling the shots! You must take responsibility for your feelings and emotions. You may have spent most of your life running away or pushing down your feelings. It is common to feel uneasy or even scared about drawing closer to your feelings, however, take notice of what happens when you move closer to them rather than trying to get away from them. Try to bring a genuine sense of curiosity to the process.

On the following page write out all the emotions that you can think of. Mind map your emotional vocabulary. Write down the name of the emotion and then around it write all the words you can attribute to it.

Name It Mind Map

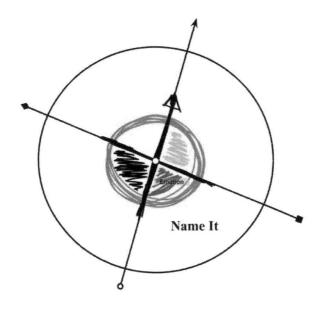

Chapter Eight

The red quadrant's simple, two-word command is "Name It." Learning and doing the command wasn't easy for me and it may be difficult for some of you. We are not taught to think about our emotions, never mind giving them a name. Usually we learn by witnessing other people's emotions and then apply a name to what we see. This is a very inaccurate way to develop our emotional vocabulary.

The actions manifested in others are not an accurate assessment of what's really going on inside of them. For example, we may see someone withdrawing or trembling. This is what we see but what is really going on inside of them? Therein lays the problem. He could be afraid, anxious, or angry but how could we truly determine his state of mind by simple observation? We can't! People who think they "know" what others are feeling are actually projecting their own emotions onto them. Emotional maturity is the ability to name what we feel. Once we have a name, then we can attempt to handle situations without unnecessarily escalating them.

While writing this chapter, my wife came into my office and we struck up a conversation about the day's events. We talked for about ten minutes then Susan appeared to become anxious and distracted. I thought to myself, "What is she feeling?" "What did I say?" "How can I help?" It turned out she needed to go to the bathroom. Simple observation is a very inadequate way of determining the emotions of others. We are very complex and difficult to read.

In Dickens' *A Christmas Carol*, the ghost of Jacob Marley asked Scrooge, "Why do you doubt your senses?" "Because," said Scrooge, "a little thing affects them. A slight disorder of the stomach makes them cheat. You may be an undigested bit of beef, a blot of mustard, a crumb of cheese, a fragment of an underdone potato. There's more of gravy than of grave about you, whatever you are!" Scrooge was right, our senses and emotions are affected by many things.

Looking back, when I first entered rehab in San Diego, I was clueless as to my own emotional state. I now know that I was running on only three emotions.

My first emotion was some version of happy when I thought things were going right for me. I guess to the outside world, outside of my head I mean, this looked very similar to everybody else's version of happy. Even though there was all that negative self-talk and never-ending PTSD reel of suicide video running in my head inside; on the outside I am sure to the world I appeared happy enough.

I sadly joked in recovery that my second emotion was stoned. This was the numbed state that my favorite drug created. In this diversionary state, my mind was in some counterfeit version of happy or joyful. As I think back, stoned was really just a fuzzy, dark cloud leading to the inevitable slide down from happy to being wounded.

It is said that the source of all addictions is pain. Is there some pain that you carry? What are your coping behaviors? How effective are they?

Chapter Eight

I used stoned to mask my third emotion: angry. When I was emotionally immature, I did not look inward. I tended to blame others for my problems or my behaviors.

My whole world prior to rehab was a mind-numbing bounce between my three states:

1. **Happy** was a thin veneer over the never-ceasing background of trauma, drama, and pain with constant recollections of my past. These memories were never good. They were always tainted with full-on shame with a healthy dose of guilt.

2. **Stoned** was a dull or checked out state that I created with chemicals to try and mask or cope with my pain and endless guilt. The trouble with stoned is that it never lasts long enough and it never really quite scratches the itch. It's a place with no promise.

3. **Angry** is a horrible place that is created when "stoned" has worn off and failed. I was left with only myself and my negative thoughts to run the whole show.

So there you have it. Those were the only tools that I had to work with for basically 30 years. What tools do you have?

One morning, early on in my recovery, I went to a group session. It was an anger management class and we were going to start working on emotions and feelings. You can imagine how excited I was. Not! I only had three miserable emotions and I didn't want to work on any of them. We were shown an Emotions wheel with eight points that looked like flower petals.

Robert Plutchik's Emotions Wheel

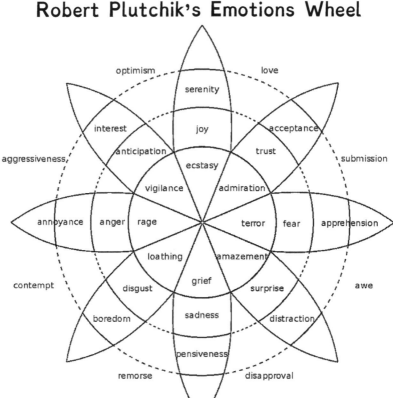

Source: Plutchik & Kellerman, 1980.

There were three circles dividing the points. The inner circle indicated that there were eight, deep, primary emotions: ecstasy, admiration, terror, amazement, grief, loathing, rage, and vigilance.[76] In the middle circle were the 8 words: joy, trust, fear, surprise, sadness, disgust, anger, and anticipation. The next circle listed: serenity, acceptance,

---

[76] Plutchik & Kellerman 1980

apprehension, distraction, pensiveness, boredom, annoyance, and interest. In the outer area were: love, submission, awe, disapproval, remorse, contempt, aggressiveness, and optimism.

While I was trying to wrap my mind around 32 emotions, the facilitators handed out a Feelings Chart that had little emoji faces printed on it. At the top of the chart, it asked the question, "Are You Aware of How You Are Feeling Now?"

I was literally stunned. Looking back at me were 70 emoji portraying a different emotion! Each little face had the name of that emotion written under it. Seventy feelings and emotions portrayed on a single piece of paper! Tears welled up in my eyes. It was beyond my comprehension that there could be so many names for what I had been feeling. I had been trying to manage my whole life with just three distorted emotions. As a matter of fact, one of the three of my emotions wasn't an emotion at all! FYI "stoned" is not an emotion!

I couldn't believe it. No wonder I couldn't express how I felt. I didn't have the names of even the basic emotions, never mind the seventy on this one piece of paper. How about you? How many emotions can you recognize and name?

Are you like I was, trying to manage your life with little or no emotional vocabulary?

On the following page, I have included the Feelings Chart directly from my recovery notebook.[77] Please take a minute and ponder these feelings and emotions.

---

[77] Source: http://www.godvertiser.com

Are You AWARE of How You Are Feeling Now?

I still have this chart. To me, it represents an absolute paradigm shift of how to manage my feelings. For the first time in my life, I started to give my feelings and emotions names, other than "happy," "stoned," or "pissed off." Now there were options to what I was feeling. I was overwhelmed! Armed with this new knowledge, I could ask the important questions, "What am I feeling?" and "Why do I feel this way?"

Check out Google for other emotional charts and articles. Don't go another day with your emotional arm tied behind your back. Unless you're in a good program like Live One Life or working with a therapist, there is nobody coming to teach you these things. It is your sole responsibility to learn the names and start to understand these many emotions so that you can deal with them.

FYI "fine" is not an emotion. When I am working with clients and I ask them, "How are you feeling?" and they answer me, "I'm fine," we're in deep trouble. I know this because in my recovery meetings we heard "fine" many times, especially in Narcotics Anonymous meetings. "FINE" is a crude yet accurate acronym for "F__d up, Insecure, Neurotic, and Emotional." It describes the feeling when your life is out of control. I don't allow "fine" as an answer in any of my counseling sessions or workshops. It's too easy of an out.

There was a man in my Anger Management class. Let's call him Charlie. Charlie was a blue-collar worker, an alcoholic and a wife beater. He had gotten into a fist fight at work with a fellow employee. His employer sent him to the class to try and salvage his job. I was still in my judgmental stage so I sat there looking down upon him. He was blue-collar; I was white-collar. He was a wife beater; I thought I was a good husband. It was pretty cut and dried in my mind.

I think it was in the second session that the facilitator said that we choose to be angry. Charlie wasn't having any of this. He said," I don't choose to be angry. It just comes before I know it." "No," the facilitator said gently, "There is a gap between what happens to you; the stimulus, and what you decide to do; the result. It is in this period of time that you get to choose."

"That's B.S.," Charlie said. "There's no time to think. I get mad and I can't help what happens after that." Charlie's logic was definitely flawed in my eyes. I thought to myself, "He has a choice. He just chooses to lash out."

Now I had always prided myself on the ability to stay cool and calm, to a point. However, once I hit that point, I thought I was no longer responsible for what happened. Now I was starting to question my own actions. Somehow this felt worse and more calculating than Charlie's impulsive behavior. I now know that I wasn't cool and calm. I was afraid of not being able to control my anger, so I stuffed it deep down and ignored it.

I was no longer concerned with Charlie's judgment calls. I was getting very concerned about my own anger management. Charlie and I were doing the exact same thing. He was choosing to go off quickly while I was choosing to go off slowly. Neither of us was very good at mastering our emotions.

The strange truth was that until that class I did not think I was angry. I had compartmentalized my emotions to the point that I couldn't find them. Observing feelings was not on my radar. If anything, I had pushed any desire to know my feelings to the farthest corner of my mind. Now I was being asked to observe my emotions like they were something tangible, as if they had the ability to influence me physically.

I remember the conversation with my therapist that shed a bright light on my emotional world.

She slipped in the words, "And David, as you come to terms with your **PTSD**..."

I exclaimed, "I don't have **PTSD**! What makes you say that?"

She asked, "David, when you were seventeen years old your father died, correct?"

I answered, "Yes."

She looked over her glasses and stated, "That was a long time ago, correct?"

"Yes," I agreed.

"Well 'now' is after that event. We call that 'post,' or after the event. Didn't you witness your father shoot himself?"

I affirmed, "Yes."

She questioned, "Do you consider that a traumatic event?"

I was starting to see where this was going and I answered, "Yes."

For clarity, she continued, "Has this caused you any stress in your life?"

"You know it has" I replied.

"I know," she stated, "you and I have discussed how that event plays over and over in a never-ending loop in your head. David, we call that a disorder; Post Traumatic Stress Disorder, or PTSD."

I was gob smacked! I just sat there trying to process what she had just said. I have PTSD!

How about you? Is there any trauma, drama or addictive behaviors from your past that might be causing you stress and manifesting itself as a disorder? Have you ever thought that you may have some form of PTSD? Now be careful here and do not self-diagnose. You are too close to your situation to be objective and may not even have the right words to describe how you feel. You might need a little "check up from the neck up" and that needs to be administered by a professional.

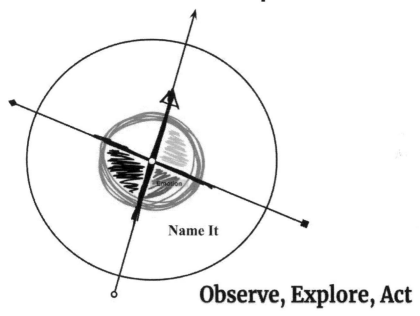

Emotions Options

Observe, Explore, Act

Observe

Becoming aware of your emotions is much easier said than done! Observing promotes mindfulness or the ability to see the emotion for what it is; without judging it or attempting to get rid of it. In rehab, we were taught to look at our emotions. At first I had no idea what this meant, however, with lots of encouragement and practice I soon became aware of how I was feeling.

Try this. Pick an emotion you are having. You may be feeling multiple emotions; pick one. Turn back to the chart, "Are You Aware of How Are You Feeling Now?" and find a name for this emotion. Now make yourself comfortable. Take 3 or 4 deep belly breaths. Do a mental scan of your body. Become conscience of each part of your body; slowly going from bottom to top. Feel the presence of your feet, your legs, your waist, and on up. Linger and notice if part of you is uncomfortable. Is there a physical sensation that is associated with this emotion? Are you frowning, are fists clenched, shoulders up to your ears, knot in your stomach, headache, or other physical pain?

Let me share another technique with you to identify your emotion. Use the blank circle below to draw the emotion right now. Can you give it a name?

Please, make an effort to work on this exercise. There is great power that comes from putting your thoughts, feelings, and emotions onto paper. Go ahead and draw an emoji of how you feel.

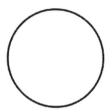

Can you give it a name? _____

Now imagine yourself moving this emotion out and away from you. Put space between you and this emotion. For the next few minutes just look at it. Notice that it's not connected to you.

With your eyes closed, answer the following questions:
If your emotion had a size, what size would it be?
If your emotion had a shape, what shape would it be?
If your emotion had a color, what color would it be?

Now I know this might sound or feel a little too new age or metaphysical for you. That's okay. Remember, we said for things to change; things really have to change. So set aside your bias and try to answer these questions.

A side note: In this book there are truly life-altering tips and techniques that may be missed in a casual reading. Go back and study the material like the exercise book it was meant to be.

Let's push forward. You should now be able to see in your mind's eye what the emotion looks like. See its' size, shape, and color. Just watch it for a few moments and recognize it for what it is. When you are ready, put it back in your body where it came from.

Take a moment to reflect on the experience. Did you notice any change in your feelings when you got a little distance from it? Continue this mindful observation on the sheets that follow. Use the mind map to record your thoughts regarding the emotion. While doing these exercises, remind yourself that you are not your emotions. You are the observer of those emotions. Name your feelings. Avoid judging. Acknowledge them, in order to learn the process of detaching from them.

Explore

During my rehab, I learned some great exercises for exploring my emotions. We were asked to examine the positive or negative sides of an emotion. For example, if you take the emotion, "anger," does it bring power and energy to you or does it just induce rage?

Compare the multiple sides of fear. Fear can provide protection and wisdom, or it can instill panic and paranoia.

- Does pain manifest itself as growth or hopelessness? You have heard it said, "No pain; no gain."
- Do you think of sadness as a healing emotion or one that just brings on melancholy or sorrow?

Look at the emotion charts and wheels in this book and try to think of the positives and negatives for each emotion. Feelings and emotions have value in your life as they teach important lessons and patience. You do not have to be a victim of the negative chemical cocktails created by your emotions.

Another exploring exercise is to determine whether you bring your emotions to particular people or situations or are your emotions induced by a particular person or situation.

There are sheets provided in this book for you to mind map your observations. Also use your personal journal. The exploration of emotions is not a one-time event. Just like picking up a guitar for a few minutes doesn't make you a guitar player. Reading about emotional exploration does not make you emotionally mature. The idea of practicing these exercises might be foreign. This is normal. Please, let go of apprehension and fear because they hold you back. These exercises will have profound effects on your life.

Don't believe every stupid thing you think! Just because you can think it, doesn't make it so. Your negative thoughts lie to you. One of the greatest tools I was taught in rehab was to see thoughts come into my mind and recognize them. If they're stupid, idiotic or destructive, ask them to leave and then watch them depart. Learning to dismiss foolish thoughts that enter your brain is a wonderful and empowering tool. I have this power and so do you!

When employing new tools and rules; remember the 3 steps to success, which are: knowledge, understanding, and application. For a principle to really work, you must first know of it, then study and understand it and finally muster up the faith to apply it to your life.

Act

You have been practicing the new art of naming, observing, and exploring emotions. Now you must decide how to act on them. Actions have real consequences for you and for others. They can get you fired, arrested, or divorced. Your emotions can help decide who you will spend the rest of your life with. Acting out on emotions can hurt loved ones and co-workers. That is why it is so crucial to differentiate behavior from internal feelings and emotions.

Actions are the manifestations of your decisions. Make these decisions based upon on your thoughts and how you observe and explore these emotions. Learning to accurately assess them is one of life's maturing exercises. Everything you initiate and exhibit stems from your thoughts and feelings. If you can slow down the execution of your thoughts and feelings, then your decisions and actions are displayed more wisely to the world.

This is what I call, "Minding the Gap." The gap is the time between stimulus and action; between a situation and how we react to it. This is where thoughts and emotions live. The better you get at observing feelings before you act, the more emotionally stable you will be.

Use the following pages to observe, explore and act out the analysis of your emotions.

Observe Mind Map

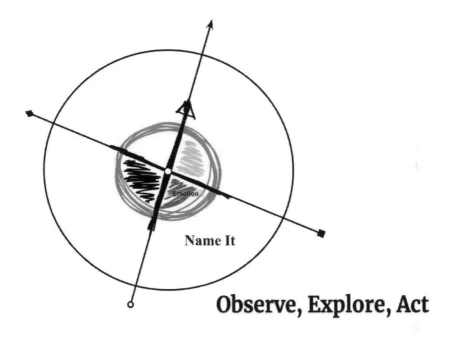

Observe, Explore, Act

Observation 5Ws

Who?   Me

What emotion will I observe?

_____

_____

_____

Where will I observe this emotion?

_____

_____

_____

When will I observe this emotion?

_____

_____

_____

Why am I observing this emotion?

_____

_____

_____

Explore Mind Map

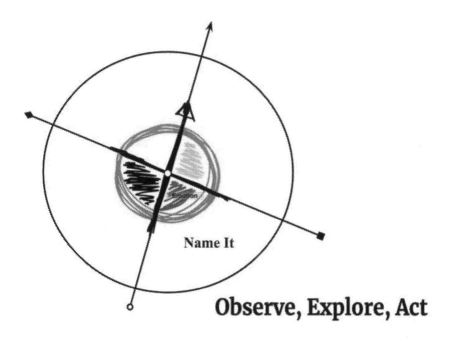

Name It

Observe, Explore, Act

Explore 5Ws

Who? Me

What emotion will I explore?

_____

_____

_____

Where will I explore this emotion?

_____

_____

_____

When will I explore this emotion?

_____

_____

_____

Why am I exploring this emotion?

_____

_____

_____

Act Mind Map

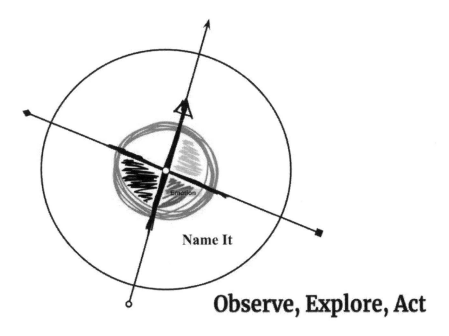

Name It

Observe, Explore, Act

Act 5Ws

Who? Me

What emotion will I act on?

_____

_____

_____

Where will I act on this emotion?

_____

_____

_____

When will I act out this emotion?

_____

_____

_____

Why am I acting out this emotion?

_____

_____

_____

It may feel strange working on emotional mind maps and 5Ws worksheets however press forward and accept the challenge. This is your work to do. There is nobody coming to straighten out your life.

Feelings and emotions have a tremendous effect on your mind, spirit and physical body. Unfortunately, you are not taught this in school and very few families ever broach the subject. The mental health system says that the following two things help the most: drugs and talk therapy. For the average person, the exercises in this book will improve your quality of life without the risks and side effects of drugs and the time and costs associated with talk therapy.

I commend you for taking the steps and working these mind maps and worksheets to help manage your own emotions. I want to be clear that if you feel you need more help, then please reach out to LiveOneLifeCoach.com or other competent mentors or professionals. Asking for help is an act of courage. Asking for help is humbly taking control.

Powerful Overarching Practices

Remember to participate daily in the powerful, overarching practices that will impact your growth in all four quadrants. They are journaling, meditation and smiling.

PTSD

Earlier in this chapter, I mentioned a conversation regarding PTSD. I would like to share with you my experience and how I used my mind, spirit, and emotions to overcome trauma and drama that resulted from my form of PTSD.

I had completed 18 months of rehab at the Kaiser Permanente Center in San Diego and I was now working again. Things were much better in my life and I had resolved many issues although there was still that never-ending suicide video of my father in my head.

It started with me grabbing my father by the arm and saying leave her alone and it ended with the shot being fired and the sound of him falling to the wooden floor. This video had run continuously in the back of my mind every waking hour of every day for over 30 years. This was the suicide loop that I was trying to erase or cope with by using drugs, alcohol, good and bad behavior, or any other kind of diversion to make it stop. Even after all my rehab, therapy and meditation, the graphic suicide video still ran continuously, unabated in my mind. I was still searching for solutions when I happened upon a CD by Anthony Robbins.

Now here is an important point. PTSD is a very serious mental illness and even potentially life threatening. If you have experienced severe trauma in your life, you should see a licensed professional who can help you with the process. Traumatic memories do not have to be a part of your every waking moment. There are many powerful techniques and experienced clinicians that can help you put the trauma in the past, where it belongs. I got excellent help from my own therapists and I share my experience here to help you find hope that you too can stop the video from looping in your mind.

On this **CD**, Tony Robbins taught a technique to erase a traumatic event. You can see this technique on YouTube; "How to Overcome Post-traumatic Stress Disorder" by Tony Robbins.[78] This technique positively changed my life forever by removing the constant replaying of my dad's suicide from my mind's eye.

Here is how I used this technique to disable the suicide video. It took me a few days to build up the courage to do it. I found a quiet place. For me, this happened to be in my car, parked alongside the road.

First, I chose my emotional anchors:

For touch, I clasped my hands in front of me.

My safe color was blue.

My safe shape was a circle.

My sound was an exhale, not quite a whistle.

My power phrase was, "Well done."

---

[78] Retrieved from
https://www.youtube.com/results?search_query=%E2%80%9CHow+to+Overcome+Post-traumatic+Stress+Disorder%E2%80%9D+by+Tony+Robbins

To establish these safe anchors just ask, "What touch feels safe?" then choose the touch. Ask, "What color represents safety to me?" Choose a color. Find a safe shape and sound. Choose your power phrase.

I took three deep breaths. I purposely viewed in my mind the sequence of events of the suicide video; noticing every detail. Be prepared because this can be painful. That's okay, you're strong enough and this is worth it.

I visualized myself sitting in a theater in a big comfortable seat with a giant screen in front of me. The images of my dad's suicide played out in a continuous loop on the screen.

Once I had that picture set in my mind, I then imagined a second David up in the projection room looking down at me as I watched the film. I watched me watching the film with great intent and paid attention to every detail. As the projectionist, I flipped the projector into reverse and watched me watch the film backwards. I then flipped it forward and sped the film up. I could see me watching a film of my dad leaving the kitchen and going to get the gun and coming back and so on, all in double time. This time I added a comic element of a monkey juggling fruit, all the while running the film forward and backward, faster and faster. Finally, I added a bear, wearing a bonnet, riding a unicycle, while it rained Jello on the entire scene. All the time I was observing as much detail as I could and running the film faster and faster backward and forward.

If at any time during this whole procedure I became fearful or anxious, I would simply change the color to blue or put a circle around the scene or say my power statement, "Well done."

I continued this until the whole scene became ridiculously absurd. It was all going so fast that it was just a blur. Then I stopped. It was quiet. I mean it was really quiet in my mind. I sat there and tried to determine what the gift was in this whole event? Then it came to me. The first gift was to my dad. He was safe and at peace. The second gift was to me. The whole experience of witnessing his suicide had made me a stronger, more independent, and ultimately a more empathetic person.

This may sound like a very strange exercise to you because I know it did to me, however, by mentally overwriting the video and changing the content, I was now in control. I was in control of the entire production! I was able to put in or take out any part of the video. I was the director and editor. This was now my video. More importantly, the old video was so damaged and corrupted it was unplayable.

This technique was life-changing for me but I do not prescribe it as a cure-all for those with trauma. Again, I had help from trained professionals and a lot of time between me and my trauma. This may not be an appropriate technique for some, especially if the trauma is fresh or happened over an extended period of time. Please consult a licensed professional trained in trauma if you are worried you are experiencing symptoms of PTSD, like vivid flashbacks.

In "10 Tips for Emotional Healing" in Psychology Today, it states: "Get a grip on your mind. Nothing causes more emotional distress than the thoughts we think. We must do a better job than we usually do of identifying the thoughts that don't serve us, disputing them and demanding that they go away, and substituting more useful thoughts. Thinking thoughts that do not serve you is the equivalent of serving yourself up emotional distress. Only you can get a grip on your own mind; if you won't do that work, you will live in distress."[79]

[79] Maisel, E. R.(2013) "10 Tips for Emotional Healing"

Chapter 9
A Body in Motion
"Treat yourself like someone you actually care about."

The lower left of my compass is the black quadrant. In the ancient aboriginal medicine wheels, this quarter represented the direction west; the season of fall; the plant is cedar; the color is black; and for our purposes, the element is our body.

All the other elements that we have discussed so far are what I call the "Inside Arts." We have learned to master and regulate our mind, spirit and emotions. Our body houses these three elements and is integrally connected and it can alter them in infinite ways. In this chapter we will learn how to master our bodies enough to thrive and accomplish the tasks of the day.

This is not the diet and exercise chapter. Heaven knows we have enough books to fill two libraries on this subject. I will talk about ways to care for your body to help in your recovery from trauma, drama, and other addictive behaviors. In times of mental, spiritual or emotional crisis, many times the first thing to be ignored or abused is our body. I know as an addict I cared less and less about my body the more intense my addiction got! Recovery itself can bring on a whole host of problems such as physical withdrawal or weight gain.

Just like in the other quadrants, I have given the body quadrant a simple, two-command. "Move It!" Move your body. There it is, the most basic of exercise programs.

When I was struggling from anxiety or depression during rehab, I could call upon this simple directive and it would change everything. I didn't need a sophisticated exercise program. I didn't need posters on my wall or a gym membership, even though all of these are great. All I needed was to remember the black quarter of my compass, "Move It." I found that the simplest of movements would help me get out of the funk that I was in.

Recent studies continue to support that exercise and activity have beneficial effects, for both physical and mental health.[80] These studies include diverse ethnic populations, including men and women, as well as several age groups.[81] You don't need a degree in physical fitness to know that exercise helps! This has been common knowledge since the 40s yet in America more than 80% of adults do not "Move It" enough to build muscle or lung capacity. In the 70s, 15% of adults were obese and now 34% are classified as obese. All this has added a staggering $150 billion-plus to our

---

[80] Blumental, Smith, & Hoffman 2012
[81] Penedo & Dahn, 2005

annual health costs.[82] I did not write this book to solve all those problems. I do want to share the simple techniques that I used and I know it will also alter your mind, spirit, and emotions.

Move It

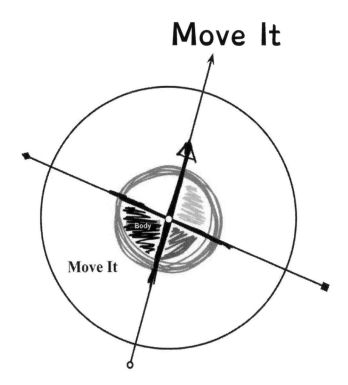

---

[82] "Facts & Statistics Physical Activity" U.S. Department of Health & Human Services

"Move It" can produce long-term health benefits. It can help:

- Prevent chronic diseases such as heart disease, cancer, and stroke (the 3 leading health-related causes of death)
- Control weight
- Make your muscles stronger
- Reduce fat
- Promote strong bone, muscle, and joint development
- Condition heart and lungs
- Build overall strength and endurance
- Improve sleep
- Decrease the potential of becoming depressed
- Increase your energy and self-esteem
- Relieve stress
- Increase your chances of living longer

It sounds like the upsides might be worth the effort!

When you are not physically active, you are more at risk for:

- High blood pressure
- High blood cholesterol
- Stroke
- Type 2 diabetes
- Heart disease
- Cancer[83]

---

[83] President's Council on Sports, Fitness & Nutrition U.S. Department of Health & Human Services

It is true that our 21st-century lifestyle does not lend itself to physical activity. Our devices keep us chained to chairs. Our cities and neighborhoods are designed for cars. Quite frankly, many of us just don't do physical work. That's not to say we are not tired. It's a different kind of exhaustion. I work with clients who are recovering from physical injuries. As they come to the end of their physical therapy and start back to work, they confuse activity with actual physical therapy. This can lead to a downhill spiral and a physical relapse to their original injury. All of us in any recovery need to analyze our activities to be sure they're beneficial to our progress.

Even though our brain only represents 2% of our body weight, it uses up 20% of our daily energy. The brain will always get what it needs. The brain doesn't care if we diminish our overall energy production with poor sleep habits, poor general exercise, poor nutrition and low water intake. It will take its energy first and leave the rest of the body with what is left. The brain is greedy and that's a good thing. Our brain keeps the lights on, our hearts beating, our lungs breathing and all the rest, 24/7.

It is your responsibility to move your body to increase energy production. "Move It" today just a little more than yesterday. Consider the 3 Ps: Patience, Progress, and Persistence! There is no need to set up an elaborate exercise program or dietary change. You know that they rarely work. What I am suggesting is just doing a little better today than you did yesterday. This should be your mantra. I really mean small changes. Park a few stalls further away from the door at work or at the store. Take the stairs, even just one flight. That's a start! It's not the amount of exertion; it's the discipline! Daily improvement over time is what will make the difference.

I was in outpatient rehab for a total of 18 months. In the first half of my rehab, I could care less about my body. As a matter of fact, I gained 50 lbs. My schedule was: rehab all day, ride the bus home, eat dinner, decompress in front of the TV, and of course being an addict, I got hooked on reruns of Law & Order. As a part of the Law & Order ritual, I would make myself peanut butter and chocolate icing sandwiches, sometimes two or three of them a night. I had no idea what the calorie count was for thick peanut butter and chocolate icing; apparently it was huge. I rationalized that the whole wheat bread was healthy!

I had developed a new coping mechanism for the stresses of life and rehab but unfortunately it wasn't a healthy one. From the very beginning of rehab, we talked about exercise and I was offered yoga classes. Somewhere in all of these personal growth classes, I finally turned the corner. I said I would sign up for yoga.

Once I started, I realized how fat and out of shape I had gotten. Just a simple stance wore me out. To make matters worse, the yoga instructor was 15 years my senior, in her late 60s. More insult to injury. I really do believe she enjoyed watching us sweat, tremble, and fall over. We tried to keep up as she performed unhuman like positions. I tried to copy the poses.

I quickly learned that coming off 20 years of prescription drug abuse doesn't lend itself to good balancing skills or flexibility. It was a physically and mentally frustrating time. I did learn that you need to have your mental, spiritual and emotional stuff together to be able to physically perform. I was becoming aware that I had to balance and grow each quadrant of my compass every day even if I was just trying a little; even if the growth was almost imperceptible.

My consistent, daily, micro steps in each quadrant were acceptable, praiseworthy and ultimately beneficial. These daily rituals were giving my brain little, positive, chemical dumps that were slowly replacing the artificial or counterfeit feel-good chemistry that came from my abuse of trauma, drama, and drugs.

In the final 8 months of rehab I was swimming every day, running on the treadmill three times a week for 1 hour, and still embarrassing myself at yoga once a week. Yes, and I did go through withdrawal from peanut butter and chocolate icing sandwiches. There is no way around the consequences of our choices. Ever!

By the time I left rehab and went back to work, I was in the best physical shape of my life. To this day, I try to do my custom version of these yoga poses and stretches every morning. I'm not as good at it as I was at the end of my rehab and that's okay. I'm doing my best every day. My mantra is **"daily improvement over time."** We all need to introduce more grace into our lives, including our physical selves.

Chapter Nine

On the next page, mind map simple ways you can move your body a little more today than you did yesterday. Map out ways that you will be consistent in your efforts. Mind map everything that comes into your brain. Write down activities and things that you will actually do and ways you will move.

Move More Mind Map

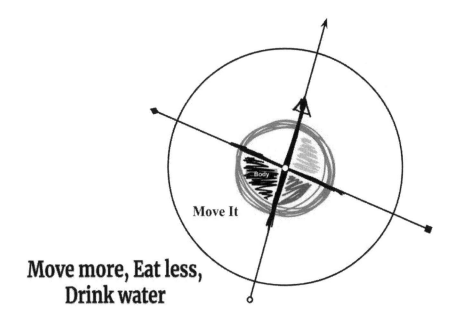

Body

Move It

**Move more, Eat less,
Drink water**

Move More 5Ws

Who? Me

What will I move more?

_____

_____

_____

Where will I move?

_____

_____

_____

When will I move?

_____

_____

_____

Why am I moving?

_____

_____

_____

Eat Less

I'm not going to get into what you can or cannot eat. I don't believe this is the problem. What you eat isn't the issue even though TV commercials and many nutritionists tell you differently. I believe it's the amount you eat, plain and simple.

Many lose sight of what food's purpose is. It is fuel and medicine for the body and should not be abused or over-indulged. I don't mean that you should never go out for a good meal with friends. I'm not saying that you can't go to the fridge for a little snack. What I am implying is that there needs to be moderation in all things. In this day and age, you definitely need to watch your intake of food and drinks. If you can grasp even a portion of that statement and live by it, your dietary concerns will almost be resolved.

Over the years, we have almost lost the word temperance. Temperance means moderation, particularly in the indulgence of natural appetites and passions. It is the opposite of gluttony and drunkenness.[84] It applies to all four quadrants of the compass and entails patience, calmness, and moderation of passion which help us recover from trauma, drama and other addictive behaviors. FYI, gluttony is #2 of the seven deadly sins. It might be worth pointing out that the word sin means "to miss the mark."[85]

---

[84] Webster, An American Dictionary of the English Language 1828
[85] Liddell, Henry George; Robert Scott, A Greek–English Lexicon, Wikipedia

Eating less involves controlling our calorie intake. According to the USDA, I need about 2500 calories a day.[86] An average man needs 2500 calories to maintain, and 2000 to lose one pound of weight per week. I tell clients how they get there, is their own business. If I want to eat 2 peanut butter and chocolate icing sandwiches a day, and nothing more, that's my choice. I don't recommend this diet, however, it is my choice and those are the calories I need.

Calorie-counting is not very effective. What I have found to be a better way to losing weight is:

1. **Wait for your stomach to growl** before you eat.
2. Remember that **your stomach is about the size of your fist,** so eat accordingly.
3. **Walk 10,000 steps a day.**

This is my simple plan. What's yours? Food is fuel. Do a little better today than you did yesterday. Remember the 3 Ps and most of all, be kind to yourself.

---

[86]www.cnpp.usda.gov/sites/default/files/usda_food_patterns/EstimatedCalorieN eedsPerDayTable.pdf

Eat Less Mind Map

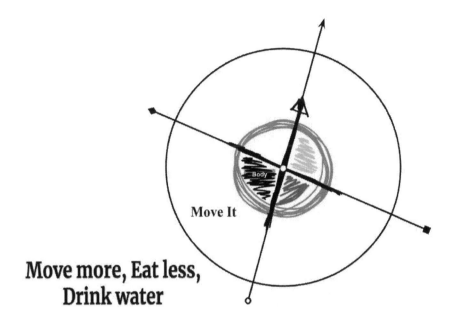

Body

Move It

**Move more, Eat less,
Drink water**

Eat Less 5Ws

Who?   Me

What will I eat less?

_____

_____

_____

Where will I eat less?

_____

_____

_____

When will I eat less?

_____

_____

_____

Why am I eating less?

_____

_____

_____

Drink Water

Okay, let's get some of the biology stuff out of the way. About 60% of your body weight is water! That should tell you to drink a lot of it. Every day you lose water through your breath, perspiration, urine and bowel movements. So how much do you need to drink to replace it? Some really smart people say about 15.5 cups (3.7 liters) of fluids for men and about 11.5 cups (2.7 liters) of fluids a day for women.[87] You've probably heard the advice, "Drink eight 8-ounce glasses of water a day." That's easy to remember and it's a reasonable goal. Most healthy people can stay hydrated by drinking water and other fluids whenever they feel thirsty.[88] I think the old adage, "Know thyself," is appropriate here. How much *you* need to stay hydrated is the most important thing. It truly does affect all four quadrants of your compass.

So how do you know if you're properly hydrated? Your fluid intake is probably adequate enough if you rarely feel thirsty and your urine is colorless or light yellow.

Other good tips from the Mayo Clinic are:

❀ Drink a glass of water or other calorie-free drink with each meal and between each meal.
❀ Drink water before, during and after exercise.

---

[87] The National Academies of Sciences, Engineering, and Medicine
[88] mayoclinic.org

🕸 Drink water if you're feeling hungry. Thirst is often confused with hunger. (Stupid brain)![89]

So there you have it, my Live One Life Health Plan.

1. Move more
2. Eat less
3. Drink water

---

[89] Homer J Simpson

Drink Water Mind Map

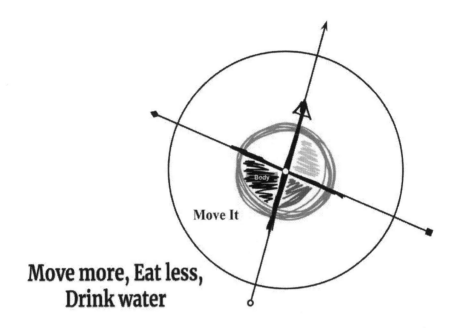

Drink Water 5Ws

Who?   Me

What will I drink?

_____

_____

_____

Where will I drink water?

_____

_____

_____

When will I drink water?

_____

_____

_____

Why am I drinking water?

_____

_____

_____

Self-Care Choices

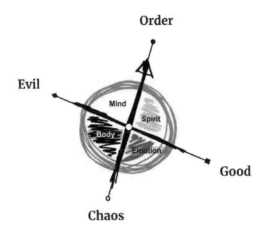

From your work on the previous pages, select an important element of the Compass that you can improve upon.

_____

_____

_____

_____

_____

_____

_____

_____

_____

_____

_____

_____

Powerful Overarching Practices

Remember to participate daily in the powerful, overarching practices that will impact your growth in all four quadrants of your compass. They are journaling, meditation, smiling, and now HALT.

HALT

At this point, I would like to introduce another overarching principle. It is the acronym HALT. It is found in almost all of the addiction fellowships. It stands for:

> **H**ungry
>
> **A**ngry
>
> **L**onely
>
> **T**ired

These are all considered weakened states. This handy acronym reminds you to take a moment (HALT) and ask yourself if you are feeling **H**ungry, **A**ngry, **L**onely, or **T**ired. It seems simple enough, yet when these basic needs are not met, you are susceptible to self-destructive behaviors including relapse. These are included in the overarching principles because they can greatly impact each of the four quadrants. HALT can serve as a reminder that you need to take care of your basic needs every day.[90]

---

[90] bradfordhealth.com

Hunger

When you are physically hungry you are truly in a weakened condition and can succumb to a variety of temptations impacting all aspects of your compass. However, you need to dig a little deeper to feel spiritual, emotional and even intellectual hunger. All of these can cause stress, anxiety, and discomfort.

You may or may not remember the ancient biblical character Esau who sold his birthright for a meal ("mess") of lentil stew ("pottage") in Genesis.[91] Some say this story is to teach you about short-sightedness and that is true. It is also true that because of his hunger, Esau was in weakened state and that was a factor in his tricky brother making that deal and cheating Esau out of the riches of his inheritance.

I have worked with clients who have destroyed many months of working on their relationship by snapping at a spouse or loved one which then escalated into a full-out, knock-down fight. Later they came to realize that they were hungry at the time. All that was needed was a little food. I'm not saying there wasn't any underlying issue that had been brewing for a long time. I am saying the fuse that set the bomb off was hunger.

Angry

Anger is a normal, healthy emotion. Your job is to slow down enough to understand what is causing your anger

---

[91] Genesis 25:29-34 KJV

and knowing how to properly express it. HALT is an awareness tool. If anger is manifesting itself then that's a sign you're not dealing with the issues.

I remember there were times during my rehab when I was angry and I didn't even know why, yet I knew I needed to deal with it. I would go to the swimming pool and put my head under water and scream as loud as I could just to release the anger. The only reason I did that is because I had been taught HALT. Better to go yell in a pool than to yell at a loved one or co-worker. If you don't have a pool, use a pillow or go clean your room. Cleaning is a very productive way of dispersing anger until you can determine what the issue is. Meditation or prayer can be a way to calm you anywhere and at any time.

Lonely

There is "being alone" and then there is "loneliness." It is important to be able to differentiate between the two. Being alone and being lonely are self-imposed situations and it is fairly easy to overcome them both. You can go out into the world and not be alone anymore. If you don't know anybody you can cure this by introducing yourself. This is called making friends! I know I have oversimplified the friend-making process, yet truth be told, this is how it's done.

Friends are like water. You need them to survive. They can help you navigate through life more easily.

I remember when I was first taught that the "L" in the acronym HALT stood for lonely. I was kind of disappointed. As an only child, being alone was kind of an old friend, however I was coming to learn that maybe it wasn't so healthy. As I look back on it, I had caused myself a lot of mischief during my life when I was alone. It was easy for me to feel alone even in a crowded room because I thought I was different than everyone else or that I had nothing in common with them. That may or may not have been true but that kind of thinking is not helpful. Using your brain to find things in common with others is a good use of gray matter. Simply go out into the world, take a walk, or run an errand, rather than hiding from everyone, or worse, returning to your traumas, dramas, and addictive behaviors.

Tired

Being tired takes a toll on your thoughts, spirit, emotions, and body. When days are full of errands, kids, and activities it is easy to disregard how tired you actually are. You compromise your capacity to manage your whole self. Taking the time to HALT is particularly critical when tired. A quick catnap can rejuvenate you physically, emotionally, and spiritually. A good night's sleep can change your outlook for the day.

When it comes to falling asleep, I have been very blessed and it drives my wife crazy. Due to a variety of physical reasons, Susan suffers from chronic insomnia. If you are in this category please seek professional help! As for me, when my head hits the pillow, I'm gone. I do keep a pen and paper next to the bed for those odd times when I do suffer from mild insomnia. When my mind starts racing, I find that writing down my issues gets them out of my head and allows my mind to rest. (Total disclosure here: these days I keep my phone next to my bed for note taking.)

As you go through various recoveries, your regular schedule may be disrupted due to pain, depression, or a new therapy. Your schedule may be taking on a mind of its own. For me, this tends to look like: sleep later during the day and stay up later at night. Ultimately if I allow it, my schedule will turn upside down! This behavior will start to mess up your circadian rhythms and ultimately mess up your recovery! Circadian rhythms are physical, mental, and behavioral changes that follow a daily cycle. They respond primarily to light and darkness. They can influence sleep-wake cycles, hormone release, eating habits and digestion, body temperature, and other important bodily functions.[92]

No matter what you are trying to change or recover from, it will be more efficient and effective if you maintain a more traditional wake and sleep cycle. It sounds corny yet the old adage, "Early to bed and early to rise makes a man healthy, wealthy and wise," really does pay off especially as you try and recover from trauma, drama, and other addictive behaviors.

There you have it. HALT is one of the most powerful overarching principles that you can employ in your life. Paying closer attention to feelings will help you prevent relapse. Take a moment throughout the day to check in with yourself. Ask, "Am I hungry, angry, lonely, or tired?"

---

[92] Circadian Rhythms, 2017, retrieved from https://www.nigms.nih.gov/education/Pages/Factsheet_CircadianRhythms.aspx

Honestly assessing how you feel takes only a minute. Doing so will make the everyday stress of life easier to deal with and help maintain the changes you are trying to implement.

Chapter 10

"Here Be Dragons"[93]

The unexplored areas on ancient maps were often marked with pictures of serpents or mythical creatures with the words, "Here Be Dragons." Making changes in your life can feel like uncharted waters and your mind can conjure up all kinds of monsters and dragons to detour you from trying. Don't be intimidated by the unknown. Know that you can tame dragons! You have come this far and you can push forward!

There is a powerful mantra that will serve you well when facing these mythical dragons! It is "If they can do it...I can do it!" Say this often, out loud with faith and hope.

"If they can do it...I can do it!"

---

[93] "Here be dragons," means dangerous or unexplored territories, in imitation of a medieval practice of putting sea-monsters and other mythological creatures on uncharted areas of maps where potential dangers were thought to exist.

Live One Life Models

I would like to recap the models that I have introduced in this book with a brief explanation of each. I will also introduce my **STEER** problem-solving model that will help you navigate through any of life's difficult situations! I will also share The Fast Track to Change, the absolute, single-most effective way to change your life!

Relationship Alignment

Relationship Alignment reminds you to be consistent in your thoughts, words, and deeds in all of your relationships in life. Most importantly, it is the integrity of your relationship between a Heavenly Father and you.

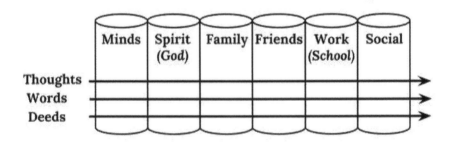

Steps of Change Model

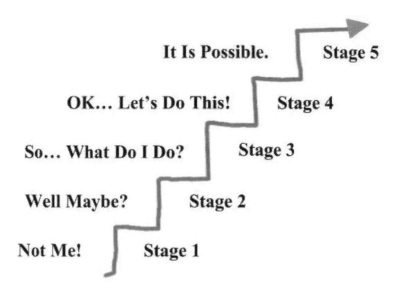

It Is Possible.   Stage 5

OK... Let's Do This!   Stage 4

So... What Do I Do?   Stage 3

Well Maybe?   Stage 2

Not Me!   Stage 1

Stage 1   Not Me!

In this stage, you are not thinking about changing and tend to defend your patterns of "trauma, drama, and other addictive behaviors." You don't see your actions as a problem. You don't understand that the positive benefits of a behavior change can outweigh the adverse consequences of continuing on the current path.

Stage 2   Well Maybe?

You are able to consider the possibility of quitting or reducing your "trauma, drama, and other addictive behaviors." However, you feel ambivalent about taking the next step because these behaviors feel enjoyable, exciting, and pleasurable. On the other hand, you may be starting to experience some adverse consequences which may include personal, psychological, physical, legal, social or family problems.

Stage 3   So...What Do I Do?

In this stage, you see the pros and cons of continuing on your current path versus taking the next move. You are willing to take some small steps toward changing your behaviors. You may start to believe that change is necessary and that the time for change is imminent. Equally, you may decide not to do anything about your behavior at this time. :-(

Stage 4   Let's Do this!

You are actively involved in taking steps to change your behaviors and are making strides toward significant progress. You may try several different techniques; however you are also at great risk of relapse. **Caution:** Ambivalence is still very likely at this stage.

Stage 5   It Is Possible.

You are now able to successfully avoid the temptations to return to your old "trauma, drama, and other addictive behavior." You have learned to anticipate and handle situations and to employ new ways of coping. You can have a temporary slip, but you don't see this as a failure.[94]

Stage 5 is the maintenance step in the 12 Step Programs; each of which has their own interpretation of recovery preservation. For now, I'll share mine.

1. Take full responsibility for **all** your actions; past and present.

2. Go public as soon as you have the courage.

3. Use your talents to share the good news of recovery.

4. Serve others who are struggling with trauma, drama, and other addictive behaviors.

5. Apply the recovery principles in this book to all aspects of your life.

---

[94] Prochaska & DiClemente, 1984

Live One Life Compass

The purpose of my Live One Life Compass is to help you quickly determine a course of recovery.

1. Do a quick self-inventory. Ask, "Which quadrants are strong and which need help now? Is it mind, spirit, emotion, or body?"

2. Decide what you want to do in this quadrant.

3. Use the simple, 2-word command and the three options for that particular quadrant. How do you want to take it from Chaos towards Order? How will you navigate comfortably between the Good and Evil options?

4. Use your mind-mapping skills to engage your course of action.

5. Once you have selected an option, the 5Ws worksheets will give you your personal plan of action to strengthen this quadrant.

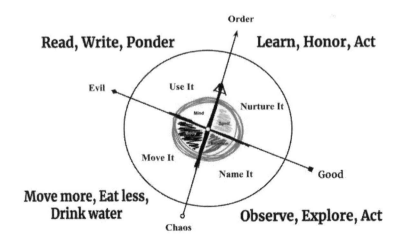

Chapter Ten

You now have an extremely detailed map and a reliable compass to change and Live One Life with meaning. Do you feel as though you are in Stage 5 It Is Possible? The map comes from the mind map exercises in each quadrant. You create custom goals. These thoughts can be reviewed and expanded using the 5Ws pages. Name specific actions you will take and apply to your life.

To orient you with your personalized goal map, choose an action item to pursue! Let's say you decided on the spiritual quadrant. The simple, 2-word command is "Nurture It." Perhaps you have decided to "Learn" more about your spiritual side. Mind map it and then complete the 5Ws questions. The answers to these questions make up your personal, detailed map directing your journey to become more spiritual.

The compass model will now help make course corrections to become more spiritual. Its function is to help make choices between Good and Evil as you pursue the details of spiritual learning. The up and to the right arrow will remind you to take your spirituality out of Chaos and bring it to some kind of Order.

The business of mind maps, 5Ws sheets, and the compass might be overwhelming at the moment. Please don't be concerned. This is absolutely normal as you're trying to make changes in your life. These are tools, any one of which will bring marked improvement. When these tools are combined and practiced over time they will become automatic. These tools assist you to become fully engaged in your own life's work.

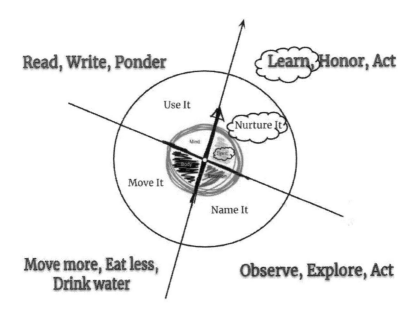

Your map and compass are not the same as modern, audible **GPS** yet with skill and practice they can become your internal voice to guide you on your journey of life.

Chapter Ten

STEER Problem Solving Model

Situations

Thoughts

Emotions

Engage

Results

"What upsets people is not things themselves; but their judgments about the things."[95]

STEER[96] is my problem-solving model. It helps navigate or **STEER** you through your problems. It helps with how you think about and respond to the world around you! The sooner you believe and understand this model the sooner you will be on your way to solving all of life's problems. I know this is a very bold statement, yet it's true.

Earlier in this book, we talked about "minding the gap." Remember, the gap was the decision between "what happened" and how you responded to "what happened." The Steer model helps you "Mind the Gap."

---

[95] "The Enchiridion" or "Handbook of Epictetus" 125 AD
[96] Ellis, 1957.

Situations are facts in your life that you don't have control over. These include people, your past, health, and the speed of traffic on the freeway or the news and current events. You don't have to go looking for situations; you just need to open your eyes in the morning and boom, there they are!

The other concept in this model that is hard to accept is that **ALL** situations are neutral. They are neither good nor bad; right or wrong, they just are! There is no judgment. Good, bad, right, or wrong are the labels that we apply to situations. This can be very difficult to acknowledge if you think you control things. In reality, you have no control over most situations. You may only have influence over them. Situations initiate your thoughts.

Thoughts are what you tell yourself about the "situation." Most think situations are facts. In reality, thoughts about situations are just your own narrative.

In the past, I assumed that when a situation happened it made me feel a certain way. This was flawed thinking! When we are exposed to a situation, our brain gives us a simple sentence to quickly explain or categorize it then *we* assign it an emotion.

Chapter Ten

Emotions are how you feel about your thoughts. If you have an adequate emotions vocabulary, you may recognize what you are feeling. There are many other emotions although these are the 8 basic ones:

> Fear
> Surprise
> Sadness
> Disgust
> Anger
> Anticipation
> Joy
> Trust

To see extreme examples of these basic emotions, spend some time watching a two-year old. They will exhibit full-blown basic emotions. Two-year olds don't try to hold back or temper their feelings. When they are afraid, they are terrified. If they are disgusted, they are over the top disgusted. If you want to see basic emotions, watch a two-year-old! How you feel about your thoughts will determine how you engage or choose to act out.

Engagement Your emotions drive how you will engage with situations and life around you. How you act is determined by your emotions. This is another difficult concept to accept. Many times you think your thoughts determine your actions. This is not true. It's really your emotions and how you *feel* that will determine what you do.

Results are generated by the way you engage in the world around you. Another way of thinking about results is that they are the consequences of your thoughts, emotions and actions; good or bad.

STEER

Situations

Can Trigger

Thoughts

Cause

Emotions

Cause

Engagement

Causes

Results

STEER Worksheet

Situations beyond your control:

_____

_____

Thoughts you assign to the situation:

_____

_____

Emotions generated by your thoughts:

_____

_____

Engagement/actions based on your thoughts & emotions:

_____

_____

Results/consequences, good or bad, from your actions:

_____

_____

The Fast Track to Change

The single most effective way to change your life is: before you go to bed, write down five things you'd like to accomplish tomorrow. Prioritize them 1-5, and then in the morning set out to accomplish them. Check them off for a "feel-good" chemical dump.

Warning: here comes a bold statement:

 This one little act, done every day, will change your life!

1. _____ ☐

2. _____ ☐

3. _____ ☐

4. _____ ☐

5. _____ ☐

12 Step Addiction Recovery Programs

Growing evidence indicates that behavioral addictions resemble substance addictions.[97] In my opinion, you can **ALL** benefit as you live the principles found in 12 Step Programs.

After all who doesn't want or need to be:

1. Honest
2. Hopeful
3. Trust in a Higher Power
4. Tell the truth
5. Admit our wrongdoings
6. Strive for a change of heart
7. Be humble
8. Seek forgiveness
9. Make restitution and reconciliation
10. Be accountable daily
11. Pray or meditate
12. Serve our fellow man[98]

I have been doing my best to live the principles ever since I seriously started my recovery. I continue to regularly use the 12 Step Addiction Recovery Program and meetings that The Church of Jesus Christ of Latter-day Saints offers through ARP.LDS.org

---

[97] Grant, Potenza, Weinstein, & Gorelick, 2010
[98] LDS Family Services, 2005

Changes Checklist

To Live One Life requires a great deal of motivation and commitment. It is necessary for you to replace old habits with new behaviors to get the most out of this program.

The following list is helpful as you start to make changes that remove traumas, dramas, and other addictive behaviors from your life.

Check all the things that you are doing regularly or have done since starting your recovery journey.

- ❏ Visit a physician for a checkup
- ❏ Schedule daily activities/goals *(The single most effective way to change your life)*
- ❏ Identify addictive behaviors *(sources of "feel-good" chemical dumps)*
- ❏ Avoid triggers (when possible)
- ❏ Destroy or remove everything you use to support your unwanted behaviors
- ❏ Avoid people who engage in your unwanted behaviors
- ❏ Avoid places of temptation
- ❏ Stop your unwanted behavior
- ❏ Use thoughts to help stop cravings
- ❏ Attend 12 Step or Mutual-help meetings
- ❏ Get a sponsor and actually work the steps
- ❏ Attend or participate in individual mentor sessions
- ❏ Discuss thoughts, feelings, and behaviors honestly with your mentor
- ❏ Exercise daily
- ❏ Pay financial obligations promptly

What other behaviors have you decided to start since you started recovery?

_____

_____

Which behaviors have been easy for you to do?

_____

_____

Which behaviors take the most effort for you to do?

_____

_____

Which behavior have you not begun yet?

_____

_____

What might need to change for you to begin this behavior?

_____

_____

While you are being tested and trying to change, do your best to represent yourself honorably and consistently "at all times, in all things, and in all places."[99] This is the essence of Living One Life.

---

[99] Mosiah 18:9

On My Office Wall

On the inside cover of my Moleskine recovery journal, I had written thoughts and highlights as they came to me during my 18 months in rehab. They were like my own personal revelations distilled down to 10 maxims. Funny how God likes the number 10.[100] Since they require total sacrifice and commitment to change, I hold them sacred. They now hang prominently on my office wall to remind me of all that I have come to know.

They are my gift to you.

Smile!

Be flexible.

God knows me.

Do your best every day.

I have all I need to succeed.

One foot in front of the other

What e're thou art, act well thy part.

If nothing changes, nothing changes.

Communication at its very best, sucks.

Attitude, gratitude and enthusiasm will overcome everything.

I contemplated how I would close this book. I thought, "The End" seemed too abrupt and I believe that the phrase, "They lived happily ever after" does not happen in this life.

---

[100] Ten Commandments

Chapter Ten

I believe we are all in a great three-act play. In the first act we lived with our Father in Heaven.[101] We are now in the second act, having come to this world and attained a body in which we are tried and tested. Finally, I believe that in the third act we will all return and report to our Father.[102] Perhaps at that time, we will hear, "They lived happily ever after."

The curtains are up.
The action is under way.
What will you do center stage?[103]

---

[101] Jeremiah 1:5 KJV

[102] 2 Corinthians 5:10 KJV

[103] "The Play and the Plan," by Boyd K. Packer on May 7, 1995

Bibliography

Adams, K. (n.d.) A short course in journal writing: It's easy to W.R.I.T.E. [Web log post]. Retrieved from https://journaltherapy.com/lets-journal/a-short-course-in-journal-writing/

Allen, J. (n.d.). As a man thinketh: The original bestseller. New York, NY: Thomas Y. Crowell Co.

Anxiety Canada, (2015, June 15). Thinking traps [PDF]. Retrieved From https://www.anxietycanada.com/sites/default/files/resources/documents/Thinking_Traps_Examples.pdf

Baikie, K. A. & Wilhelm, K. (2005). Emotional and physical health benefits of expressive writing. Advances in Psychiatric Treatment, 11 (5), 338 – 346.

Beard, L. (2018). Freedom from self-slavery: The 7 Rs method: A guide for self-mastery and empowerment. Published by Amazon Digital Services LLC

Belomancy, (n.d.). In Wikipedia. Retrieved from https://en.wikipedia.org/wiki/Belomancy

Berns, G. S., Blaine, K., Prietula, M. J., & Pye, B. E. (2013). Short- and long-term effects of a novel on connectivity in the brain. Brain Connect, 3(6), 590 – 600.

Bite-sized Philosophy (2017, May 10). Jordan Peterson – I act as if God exists [Video file]. Retrieved from https://www.youtube.com/watch?v=UKG4_psaC9k

Blumenthal, J. A., Smith, P. J., & Hoffman, B. M. (2012). Is exercise a viable treatment for depression? ACSM's Health & Fitness Journal, 16(4), 14.

Bremner, J. D. (2006). Traumatic stress: effects on the brain. Dialogues in clinical neuroscience, 8(4), 445 – 461.

Circadian rhythms (2017). Retrieved from https://www.nigms.nih.gov/education/Pages/Factsheet_CircadianRhythms.aspx

Color meaning (n.d.). Retrieved from //www.color-wheel-pro.com/color-meaning.html

Covey, S. R. (2013). The 7 habits of highly effective people: Powerful lessons in personal change. New York, NY: Simon & Schuster.

Ellis, A. (1957). Rational psychotherapy and individual psychology. Journal of Individual Psychology, 13, 39 – 44.

Grant, J. E., Potenza, M. N., Weinstein, A., & Gorelick, D. A. (2010). Introduction to behavioral addictions. The American Journal of Drug and Alcohol Abuse, 36(5), 233–241.

Heinz, A. J., Disney, E. R., Epstein, D. H., Glezen, L. A., Clark, P. I., & Preston, K. L. (2010). A focus-group study on spirituality and substance-user treatment. Substance Use & Misuse, 45(1-2), 134–153.

Hill, P. L., Allemand, M., & Roberts, B. W. (2013). Examining the pathways between gratitude and self-rated physical health across adulthood. Personality and individual differences, 54(1), 92 – 96.

iMindMap. (2015, January 26). How to mind map with Tony Buzan. [Video file]. Retrieved from https://www.youtube.com/watch?v=u5Y4plsXTV0&feature=youtu.be

Ireland, D. (2015, December 11). Medicine wheel teachings [Web log post]. Retrieved from http://archaeologymuseum.ca/medicine-wheel-teachings/

Jason Stephenson – Sleep Meditation Music. (2016, March 21). Spoken meditation for addiction: Help for substance, gambling, alcohol, drugs, depression, asmr [video file]. Retrieved from https://www.youtube.com/watch?v=a8_ENeZ2x28

Bibliography

Kidd, D. C. & Castano, E. (2013). Reading literary fiction improves Theory of Mind. Science, 342 (6156), 377 – 380.

Krisciunas, K. (2013). A guide to wider horizons. Published by Kendall Hunt Publishing

Krpan, K. M., Kross, E., Berman, M. G., Deldin, P. J., Askren, M. K., & Jonides, J. (2013). An everyday activity as a treatment for depression: the benefits of expressive writing for people diagnosed with major depressive disorder. Journal of affective disorders, 150(3), 1148–1151.

LDS Family Services. (2005). Addiction recovery program: A guide to addiction recovery and healing. Salt Lake, UT: The Church of Jesus Christ of Latter-day Saints.

Lewis, C. S. (1986). Mere Christianity. New York, NY: Simon & Schuster.

Maisel, E. R. (2013, September 16). 10 tips for emotional healing [web log post]. Retrieved from https://www.psychologytoday.com/us/blog/rethinking-mental-health/201309/10-tips-emotional-healing

Melemis, S. M. (2010). I want to change my life: How to overcome anxiety, depression and addiction. Published by Modern Therapies

Narcotics Anonymous World Services. (1992). Just for today: Meditations for recovering addicts. Revised edition. Los Angeles, CA: Narcotics Anonymous

Packer, B. K. (1995). The play and the plan. Kirkland Washington Stake Center, The Church of Jesus Christ of Latter-day Saints, Kirkland, WA.

Penedo, F. J., & Dahn, J. R. (2005). Exercise and well-being: a review of mental and physical health benefits associated with physical activity. Current Opinion in Psychiatry, 18(2), 189-193.

Peterson, J. B. (2018). 12 rules for life: An antidote to chaos. Toronto, Canada: Random House

Peterson, J. B. (2017). The psychological significance of the Biblical stories [video file]. Retrieved from https://jordanbpeterson.com/bible-series/

Peterson, J. B. (2017). Redefining reality [Video file]. Retrieved from https://www.youtube.com/watch?v=HgP7yZBWSmw

Plutchik, R. & Kellerman, H. (1980). Emotion: Theory, research, and experience. Volume 1: Theories of emotion. New York, NY: Academic Press.

Prochaska, J. O. & DiClemente, C. C. (1984). Self-change processes, self-efficacy, and decisional balance across five stages of smoking cessation. In Advances in Cancer Control. New York, NY: Alan R. Liss, Inc.

Protas, A., Brown, G., Smith, J., & Jaffe, E. (2001). Dictionary of symbolism — Circle Entry [Web log post]. Retrieved from http://umich.edu/~umfandsf/symbolismproject/symbolism.html/C/circle.html

Rodriguez, T. (2013, November, 1). Writing can help injuries heal faster [Web log post]. Retrieved from https://www.scientificamerican.com/article/writing-can-help-injuries-heal-faster/

Seven Spiritual Needs (n.d.) [Web log post]. Retrieved from https://www.takingcharge.csh.umn.edu/create-healthy-lifestyle/life-purpose-and-spirituality/what-life-purpose/seven-spiritual-needs

Ullrich, P. M. & Lutgendof, S. K. (2002). Journaling about stressful events: Effects of cognitive processing and emotional expression. Annals of Behavioral Medicine, 24(3), 244 — 250.

Velicer, W. F., Prochaska, J. O., Fava, J. L., Norman, G. J., & Redding, C. A. (1998). Smoking cessation and stress management: Application of the Transtheoretical Model of behavior change. Homeostasis, 38, 216 — 233.

Webb, C. H. (2017, June). Faith as a principle of action and power. Seminaries and institutes of religion annual training broadcast. The Church of Jesus Christ of Latter-day Saints, Salt Lake City, UT.

Webster, N. (1828). American dictionary of the English language. Printed by Hezekiah Howe

White, T. (n.d.) How big is the candle industry? [Web log post]. Retrieved from https://smallbusiness.chron.com/big-candle-industry-69541.html

World Science Festival. (2016, November 15). What's harder to understand, a human brain or the universe? [Video file]. Retrieved from https://www.youtube.com/watch?v=pA41aRN04f4

Wooden, J. & Carty, J. (2009). Coach Wooden's pyramid of success. Grand Rapids, MI: Revell

Ziglar, Zig. (2000). See you at the top: 25th anniversary edition. Carrollton, TX: Pelican Publishing

About the Author

Dr. David Patterson received his Doctorate of Divinity from Trinity International Seminary, Dallas TX. He has been coaching and counseling people in the church and business community for over 35 years. His life experience and training have uniquely equipped him to be able to empathize and quickly understand difficult issues and situations.

David is a survivor. He has overcome the frustrations of undiagnosed dyslexia, worked through PTSD as a result of witnessing his father's suicide, and recovered from a 20-year addiction to prescription drugs. He is also a cancer survivor. David is a coach who has truly, "Been there, done that!"

He brings a keen sense to the pressures of personal trauma, drama, and addictions in his peer to peer coaching style. Dr. Patterson is a sensitive, challenging, and pragmatic coach using techniques that work.

His book, "Live One Life; A Guide to Recovery from Trauma, Drama, and Other Addictive Behaviors" is the centerpiece of his practice. Using his "Live One Life Compass" and "Relationship Alignment" models, he will help you find your strength, develop pain management skills, and restore confidence by balancing your mind, spirit, emotions and body.

Dr. Patterson's own life and service as a Life Coach and church leader have prepared him to assist you in finding and restoring your life's purpose. His passion is to help people understand their destination so that they can "Live One Life" joyfully.

Contact:
Dr. David W. Patterson
www.LiveOneLifeCoach.com
liveonelifecoach@gmail.com

55554673R00124

Made in the USA
Columbia, SC
15 April 2019